Stefan Buczacki

Best Geraniums

Special Photography Andrew Lawson

HAMLYN

Publishing Director Laura Bamford
Creative Director Keith Martin
Design Manager Bryan Dunn
Designer TT Designs
Executive Editor Julian Brown
Editor Karen O'Grady
Production Julie Hadingham
Picture Research Liz Fowler
Researcher Liz Dobbs
Special Photography Andrew Lawson

First published in Great Britain in 1998
by Hamlyn
an imprint of Reed Consumer Books Limited
Michelin House, 81 Fulham Road,
London SW3 6RB
and Auckland, Melbourne, Singapore and Toronto

© Reed Consumer Books Limited 1998
Text © Stefan Buczacki 1998
Design © Reed Consumer Books Limited 1998

Produced by Toppan
Printed in China

A catalogue record for this book is available from
the British Library

ISBN 0 600 59371 1

CONTENTS

M. West

April 2008

GENERAL INTRODUCTION

The Plant Kingdom is divided by botanists into families, each of which is believed to embrace plants that have a natural relationship with each other. Families are sub-divided into genera which have more clearly recognised similarities, and then species. These relationships are most obvious in the detailed structure of the flowers, and leaves, stems and roots have little bearing on the groupings; plants in different families may have similar leaves. So it is because of a similar flower shape that a group of fourteen plant genera are brought together in the family *Geraniaceae*. Like many other large families, there are sub-groups of

genera (sub-families) that contain plants that are more closely related to each other than they are to other parts of the family. It is within one of these sub-families (*Geranioideae*) that the family's three most widely cultivated ornamental genera are placed: *Geranium*, *Pelargonium* and *Erodium*. The first two of these are the subject of this book and together they account for about 600 (roughly 300 each) of the total of 730 species in *Geraniaceae*.

I have to confess that I have spent many years reminding gardeners that there is a difference between *Geranium* and *Pelargonium*, and that the common name of 'geranium' is not interchan-

geable. However, I have decided to call this book *Best Geraniums* for the sake of simplicity.

The most practical difference between *Geranium* and *Pelargonium* is that most species of *Geranium* are hardy in temperate climates such as the UK and can be grown outdoors all year round; most species of *Pelargonium* will not tolerate frost and must be taken under cover in winter. To a botanist the distinction lies mainly in the flowers of *Geranium* being regular in shape – the five petals are of the same size and shape; those of *Pelargonium* are lop-sided – the upper two petals are distinct from the lower three.

Pelargonium 'Polka'

4

Both genera have been popular in British gardens for a very long time. Of course *Geranium* has the longer cultivated history in European gardens because many species are native to Europe or adjacent areas. The growing of several must date from that grey area in horticultural history when ancient peoples simply encouraged the local vegetation to grow close to their homes, even if they did not deliberately garden. And it was obviously a European species of *Geranium* (although which is unknown) to which the Greek physician Dioscorides was referring when he used the name *geranos*. This is the Greek word for crane and refers to the shape of the seed pod which resembles the shape of that bird's beak. Even today the now rather infrequently used common name for geraniums is cranesbills. But ancient as their cultivation is, it was the opening up of China and the Himalayas to western exploration in the nineteenth century, and the steady flow of new species from these areas that gave a huge impetus to *Geranium* growing.

Most *Pelargonium* species are native to South Africa and it was not until the trading ships of the East India Company called there on their way back to Europe that South African plants first appeared in Europe. The first pelargonium to be seen in Europe was probably *Pelargonium zonale* which was certainly present in Holland, as the gift of the Governor of Cape Colony, in 1609. The number of introductions increased over the succeeding years and, by early in the eighteenth century, the parent species of most of the important garden groups of pelargoniums had arrived in Europe. Perhaps

Geranium subcaulescens

the greatest, although generally unrecognised fillip that pelargonium cultivation in Britain had, was in 1845 when the much despised Glass Tax was finally repealed and greenhouse manufacture plummeted in cost, allowing more people to grow tender plants.

It is scarcely possible to imagine our summer gardens today without geraniums and pelargoniums, although (or perhaps because) in some ways, they represent two different styles of gardening. The modern garden *Geranium* is still recognisably close to the wild species from which it is derived. Indeed, I can think of rather few other groups of border perennial in which we grow quite so many true species and relatively so few varieties. This 'naturalness', for want of a better term, endears them particularly to the enthusiast for wild, cottage and informal gardening. On many occasions in this book, I have mentioned the 'wild' garden as an appropriate place for a particular geranium type.

By contrast, the garden *Pelargonium* is a highly hybridised, selected and altered creature. In a relatively short number of years, a mere handful among the

three hundred species has given rise to a huge number of varieties; over 3,000 are currently available. There is little natural about them, and in their bold, often garish colours, they are quite alien to informal gardening. They find their home in the window box, hanging basket and other containers of the modern, much more structured garden.

Together, the two groups are invaluable to gardeners, but because of their important differences, I have given quite separate introductions to their use and cultivation. In my choice of recommended varieties, I have, as always in this series, limited myself to plants that I think I know something about. I have grown a considerable proportion of them over the years but to help you decide which to choose for your own garden, I have indicated those varieties that have been granted the AGM (Award of Garden Merit) of the Royal Horticultural Society. While this is not a guarantee that you will succeed with a plant or even like it, an AGM does at least denote those plants that have achieved recognition, by experts, for their garden value.

Geraniums

Geraniums are among the easiest of hardy herbaceous perennials to grow. I am sure this is largely because they are little changed from the wild species, and the natural habit, at least of most of the European types, can be met in British gardens. If you have a medium, well-drained loam of around pH 7 (more or less neutral), you will succeed with every geranium that I mention. If your soil is wetter and heavier, drier and lighter, or more or less acid than this, you may find that some do better than others. Therefore let us look briefly at these 'alternative' soils and how they should be managed.

Soil and Site

All soils contain greater or lesser amounts of sand, silt, clay and humus; it is their relative proportions that give each soil type its characteristic features. A soil with a high clay content will be slow to warm up in spring but then retains warmth well and is likely to be generously supplied with nutrients. In dry conditions, however, it can be hard and impenetrable, whereas in wet winter weather, it may become waterlogged. To succeed in this soil, choose those geraniums like *Geranium sylvaticum*, *Geranium palustre* and *Geranium wallichianum* and varieties derived from them, that grow naturally close to stream-sides or in damp woodland. By contrast, a light sandy soil will warm up quickly, cool down quickly and, being free-draining, lose both water and nutrients rapidly. The greatest success here will generally come from species like *Geranium sanguineum* that grow on thin, free-draining hill-side soils, but you will also find that those that are naturally plants of mountain screes and similar habitats, plants like *Geranium cinereum* and *Geranium orientalitibeticum* also thrive well.

ABOVE: *Geranium sanguineum* var. *striatum*

RIGHT: *Geranium cinereum* 'Lawrence Flatman'

To amend your soil, in order to succeed better with those geraniums that do not naturally have an affinity with your soil, you should turn to humus – partly-decomposed organic matter. This will improve both light and heavy soils because it contains natural 'glues', binding together soil particles to form crumbs and help the soil retain moisture. And even if you feel that your soil is ideal for your choice of geranium, always dig in plenty of compost, manure or other organic matter before planting because this will invariably aid initial root establishment.

I have already hinted at another aspect of soils that you may need to take into account, its relative acidity or alkalinity. In reality, this is far less of a problem with geraniums than with many other types of garden plant but if your soil is very strongly alkaline, (above pH 8.5) then *Geranium sanguineum*, with its natural home on chalk and limestone is the best to try. Most geraniums will also succeed in fairly acidic soils, although very strong acid conditions (below pH 5.5) are those that are least suitable.

Aspect is perhaps more important than soil type. Some geraniums, such as *Geranium sylvaticum* and particularly *G. phaeum* and its relatives, are woodland plants and will be those most likely to succeed in shade. In practice they are among the best and most reliable herbaceous perennials for a shaded or woodland area; *G. phaeum* and *G.* x *monacense* grow in rather dense shade in my own garden. Most other geraniums will tolerate lightly dappled shade, although the bulk of them, and certainly the alpine species, grow better and will flower better in full sun.

Above: *Geranium macrorrhizum* 'Ingwersen's Variety'   **Right:** *Geranium pratense* 'Plenum Violaceum'

Care

The geraniums in my garden require no special feeding, no special watering and no special winter protection; in all these respects they are among the easiest of the herbaceous perennials that I grow. Feed your geraniums with your other herbaceous perennials in the spring. I adopt slightly different feeding for what I think of as the two main subdivisions in terms of their garden role. The normal border species, be they ground cover types such as *Geranium macrorrhizum* or upright, bushy plants such as *Geranium psilostemon*, are given a general fertiliser such as fish, blood and bone as growth begins in the spring, and then given a second dose as the flowers fade. The Alpine-type species are fed at exactly the same time, but I find they thrive better with bone meal which contains less nitrogen.

Some geraniums, because they are rather shallow-rooted and soft-stemmed, suffer quickly in very dry weather, and thorough watering, followed by mulching in the spring, is important in enabling them to cope with these periods. I always try to deadhead, (cutting back entire flowering stems) as the flowers fade; this makes for a more tidy plant but also encourages a number of species to flower again later in the season.

The important way in which I find geraniums, at least the border species, do need special attention is in staking and support. Very few geraniums have stems that are stout enough not to flop in the border. Looking at my own collection, I suppose that the *Geranium phaeum* group and *Geranium psilostemon* are among the more reliable. Certainly, with *Geranium pratense* and *Geranium wallichianum*, flopping is the order of the day. Single stakes do not work effectively because the clumps are too broad, and the solution really lies between what I call 'wrap-around' and 'grow-through' support. The wrap-around type may take the form of four or five canes placed at the sides of the clump, with green string lightly tied around them, or purpose-made metal, 'L'-shaped interlocking stakes. The grow-through approach is provided by metal grid-pattern discs attached to vertical supports (although I find that the plants are forever trying to push the grid off its supports), or small twiggy branches, a prettier alternative. But whichever pattern you adopt, put the support in place early, before the stems really begin to elongate.

Propagation

All garden geraniums can be easily propagated by division. And some are such vigorous growers that annual division is necessary to keep the plant in check. Some species, especially ground-covering sorts, routinely root at the surface, and the rootstock is raised above soil level. I find it best to replant these every two or three years or they will become untidy. Many geraniums grow true to type from seed and this is easily obtained from the brown seed pods which should be collected before they explode and discharge their contents. I sow the fresh seed in soil-based sowing compost and keep the pots in a cold frame over the winter. Seed then tends to germinate erratically, but fairly surely, over a period of several months. However, many geraniums, including the species, are variable and plants you obtain from seed may not be as good as the parent. Stem cuttings of many types will root fairly readily if taken in early summer, as will root cuttings taken in autumn.

Pests and Diseases

Fortunately, most geraniums are fairly free from pests and diseases. Geranium rust, which causes brown, black or orange pustules on the undersides of the leaves, is the only major disease but it is rarely severe and can be controlled by spraying with a fungicide containing penconazole. Pests may be slightly more troublesome, and whitefly can be a problem on *Geranium maderense* and related species. The fleshy-rooted species may be attacked by slugs and other subterranean pests, while I have found some of the low-growing geraniums, and especially *Geranium himalayense* 'Plenum' are attacked by small leaf-eating beetles of flea beetle type.

RIGHT: *Geranium maderense*

BELOW: *Geranium himalayense*

USING GERANIUMS IN THE GARDEN

Geraniums are versatile garden plants, and there is a species or variety for most situations, although there are some ways in which I find they are particularly successful. Let's look first at their most obvious role, in the herbaceous border. All of the bushy species are valuable, but most are tall enough only for what I would call the front to centre position. The tallest that I grow, *Geranium psilostemon*, will hold its own in the middle of the border but none are tall enough for the back. The mass of lovely, but rather floppy species and varieties, like 'Johnson's Blue' and *G. wallichianum* 'Buxton's Variety' are better grown almost at the front. And in front of these can be planted the many types that span the boundary between border and alpine garden plants; plants such as *Geranium cinereum* and *Geranium orientalitibeticum*. In the mixed border too, geraniums are valuable but bear in mind that many thrive best in the sun and be careful not to plant them in too much shade, near large shrubs. The few shade-loving species, most notably *Geranium phaeum* and its relatives, among the taller types, and to a lesser degree, *Geranium*

Geranium asphodeloides

macrorrhizum among the ground cover forms, are invaluable in either a border that receives little sun, or in the woodland garden.

Perhaps some of the loveliest plants to associate with geraniums are roses, especially old roses. This works because, like clematis (see *Best Clematis*), their colours, in shades of pink, mauve, purple and white, in most instances, blend particularly well. But, as with other shrubs, do heed my warning not to plant the geraniums so close to the roses that they are shaded by them. You will find a wide range of rose varieties, both old and modern, grouped by colours in *Best Roses*.

While the hardy geranium is one of the archetypal plants of the border, I think that the greatest merits of the genus may lie with the low-growing, more or less alpine species. Grow these in an alpine bed, in troughs or, perhaps best of all, in a raised bed where their attractive flowers and foliage are closer to view, and you will add a very appealing extra dimension to your rock garden plantings. Not least of the benefits is that geraniums begin to flower at the time when many other alpines are fading.

Although a number of garden plants will 'turn' on their owners, and become a nuisance in time, the only geranium that I have nearly regretted planting is *G.* x *oxonianum* 'Claridge Druce'. It self-seeds with a genuine fury, although there are a few others (that I have studiously avoided) of which this is also true, and they too can bring problems to small spaces. I have indicated such plants in the text. The tuberous species (page 33) can also spread rapidly and need to be watched carefully. However,

I have never experienced a problem with any geranium simply through the invasiveness of a single plant, only through the spread of seedlings.

There are two other important considerations when planting most types of hardy geranium. The first is that the majority have a relatively short flowering season, although most can be encouraged to produce a smaller, second flush of bloom later in the season if they are dead-headed (page 9). In Britain and most other parts of Europe, the majority of geraniums begin to flower in early summer and continue for a few weeks. Among the commonly available types that usually begin to flower in spring are *G. eriostemon, G. libani, G. macrorrhizum, G. maculatum, G. phaeum, G. sylvaticum* and *G. tuberosum.* Among the few that begin to flower later in the summer are

G. procurrens, G. thunbergii and *G. wallichianum.*

The second important feature is that of colour. The majority of geraniums have strong colours, indeed that is part of their appeal, but these are limited to a range from rich purple-mauve, through lilac and pink to blue, with white forms occurring in many species. As with any other type of garden plant, it is important to blend these colours carefully and as I have indicated above, the colours of many geraniums blend well with the colours of old roses. In practice, the only problematic colours that I have found in geraniums come with the magentas and pinks. The magenta of *G. psilostemon* and *G. cinereum* ssp. *subcaulescens* 'Giuseppii' are fierce indeed and must be positioned carefully, as should the pink of varieties like *Geranium sanguineum* 'Shepherd's Warning'.

Geranium renardii

GERANIUM ENDRESSII AND RELATED TYPES

" *Many gardeners have been introduced to geranium growing by 'Wargrave Pink', a strong-growing, ground-covering plant with one of the best shades of pink in the entire genus. It is an excellent variety with an AGM, and it demonstrates the inestimable value of a nurseryman with keen eyes because it was found, not deliberately raised, at the old Waterer nursery in the late 1920s by their foreman. It should encourage further exploration of the* G. endressii *group, which embraces four species, and their hybrids, from Southern Europe and western Asia. If your real affection is for* G.endressii *itself, however, try the less vigorous 'Castle Drogo'.* "

Geranium endressii

Geranium endressii

ORIGIN: Pyrenees, cultivated in gardens since 1812. A strong coloniser that has become naturalised both in southern Europe and further north.
SITE AND SOIL: Thrives in sun or shade. Tolerates most soils although moist conditions will give the best display.
HARDINESS: Very hardy, tolerating -20°C (-4°F).
SIZE: 45 x 60cm (18 x 24in).

SPECIAL FEATURES

Long-flowering evergreen. Excellent ground cover in moderate shade or as an edging to a border. Readily hybridizes with other species.

Recommended Varieties:

G. endressi (AGM), bright pink, long-flowering; 'Castle Drogo', mid-pink, slow spreading habit; *G. e. album*, white.

'Kate' (syn. 'Kate Folkard'), a hybrid of *G. endressii* and *G. sessiliflorum* named after the daughter of the Rev. O G Folkard who found it in his garden in Sleaford, Lincolnshire in the 1970s. At only 10-15cm (4-6in) high, with a trailing habit, it is ideal for a rock garden or for neat ground cover. The flowers are pale pink with darker veins and the foliage is bronze.

'Prestbury Blush' (syns. *G. endressii* 'Prestbury White', *G. x oxonianum* 'Prestbury White'), palest pink.

Geranium nodosum

ORIGIN: Mountain woods from central France to the Pyrenees, also central Italy and former Yugoslavia, introduced to gardens in 1633. Its relative *G. versicolor* is from central and southern Italy, Sicily, Greece, former Yugoslavia and Albania and was one of the earliest geraniums to be cultivated in gardens and introduced to Britain from Italy in 1629.
SITE AND SOIL: *G. nodosum* and *G. versicolor* tolerate medium shade and *G. nodosum* is also tolerant of dry conditions.
HARDINESS: Very hardy, tolerating -20°C (-4°F).
SIZE: 45 x 45cm (18 x 18in).

SPECIAL FEATURES

G. nodosum and *G. versicolor* are not spectacular, but can add interest under trees in wild or woodland gardens. Forms of *G. nodosum* offer continuous flowers for dry shade, but should not be planted close to *G. endressii* if you wish to keep the stock pure, as they hybridize readily.

Recommended and Similar Forms:

G. nodosum, lilac, glossy green foliage, will self-seed freely; 'Svelte Lilac' (syn. 'pale form'), lilac with red veins; 'Swish Purple' (syn. 'dark form'), violet-purple with darker veins, foliage darker and more divided; 'Whiteleaf', pale purple with a silver sheen to the flowers.
G. versicolor, white with magenta veins, self-seeds freely, brown-blotched foliage.

Geranium x *oxonianum* 'Wargrave Pink'

Geranium x oxonianum

ORIGIN: A range of hybrids between *G. endressii* and *G. versicolor*.
SITE AND SOIL: Tolerates both sun and shade. Successful on most soils, even dry sites if given moisture and organic matter to aid initial establishment.
HARDINESS: Very hardy, tolerating -20°C (-4°F).
SIZE: At least 45-60 x 60cm (18-24 x 24in).

SPECIAL FEATURES

Most of the numerous hybrids are fertile but many do not make good garden plants. However, the following named forms are worth growing if sufficient space is available because most are taller than either parent and have larger flowers. Easy to grow in open positions. Their evergreen leaves make a weed-smothering ground cover or alternatively, they may be allowed to scramble through shrubs.

Geranium x *oxonianum* 'Claridge Druce'

Recommended Varieties

'A. T. Johnson', light silver-pink, although some plants sold under this name have salmon-pink flowers; 'Claridge Druce', deep rose-pink with darker veins, very vigorous, seeds freely although seedlings show considerable variation. I made the mistake of planting it in too small an area and have lived to regret it; 'Frank Lawley', a recent introduction with large salmon-pink flowers, low growing; 'Hollywood', pale pink with darker veins; 'Kate Moss', pale blush pink; 'Lace Time, white with magenta veins; 'Lady Moore', deep pink-purple with darker veins, very vigorous, blotched foliage; 'Miriam Rundle', deep red-purple, relatively small;

'Old Rose', flowers change colour as they age from deep pink to red-purple, prominent veins; 'Rebecca Moss', near-white deepening to pale pink; 'Rose Clair', rose-pink with faint veins, buy plants in flower because *G. versicolor* is often sold under this name; 'Rosenlicht', red-purple; 'Sherwood', pale pink, narrow petals and petaloid stamens which give the appearance of extra petals; 'Southcombe Double', neater than most of the hybrids at only 15cm (6in) tall, small, deep salmon-pink flowers with petaloid stamens giving a double-flowered effect; 'Southcombe Star', blue-pink flowers, narrow petals, similar to 'Southcombe Double' but less

compact; 'Thurstonianum' (syn. *G. thurstonianum*), purple, very narrow petals and petaloid stamens can give the effect of semi-double flowers, some plants have blotched foliage, buy plants in flower because many different forms are sold under this name; 'Wageningen', bright salmon-pink, like 'Wargrave Pink' but more intense and doesn't blend as readily with other varieties; 'Walter's Gift', small flowers of pale pink with darker veins, dark reddish markings on foliage; 'Wargrave Pink' (AGM), bright salmon-pink, a very popular, although very vigorous, weed-suppressing cover; 'Winscombe', very pale silver-pink flowers that deepen with age to give a two-tone effect.

Geranium x riversleaianum

ORIGIN: Arose as the result of a cross between *G. endressii* and *G. traversii* (a New Zealand species – see page 28).
SITE AND SOIL: Best in full sun but thrives in most good soils.
HARDINESS: Hardy, tolerating -15°C (5°F).
SIZE: 23-45 x 90cm (9-24 x 36in).

SPECIAL FEATURES

A flowering carpet which dies back in winter. The following varieties are useful for their long flowering period.

BELOW LEFT: *Geranium* x *riversleaianum* 'Mavis Simpson'

BELOW: *Geranium* x *riversleaianum* 'Russell Prichard'

Recommended Varieties: 'Mavis Simpson', shell pink with darker veins; 'Russell Prichard' (AGM), bright magenta-pink, a very popular variety but best if you protect the crown in winter and divide it regularly in spring. *G.* 'Little Gem' (*G. oxonianum* x *G. traversii*), is similar to 'Russell Prichard' with smaller, but more intense, magenta flowers.

GERANIUM SYLVATICUM AND RELATED TYPES

❝ *I am constantly surprised at how much interest people have in knowing which are my favourite plants in any particular group. And because it is as true of geraniums as any others, I have to reveal that, so short a way into the book, you've already arrived at one of them.* Geranium sylvaticum *may not be the one I love above all others, but it's certainly my favourite among native British species. Having seen all of our native geraniums growing in their natural habitats, none gave me as much pleasure as my first sight of* Geranium sylvaticum *growing at the edge of damp woodland close to the High Force waterfall in Upper Teesdale, that glorious and botanically rich area of northern England. Even among a genus of fine colours, its flowers are of a very special shade, one that, on my first acquaintance, and I have thought ever since, is enhanced by dappled light filtering through a tree canopy. It looks right in a wood; and it isn't called* sylvaticum *(meaning 'of woods') for nothing.* ❞

Geranium sylvaticum

ORIGIN: A native of most of Europe and also northern Turkey occurring in damp meadows, river banks, lightly shaded woods and roadsides.
SITE AND SOIL: Tolerates sun or light shade. Any reasonable garden soil is suitable but thrives best in soils that do not dry out.
HARDINESS: Very hardy, tolerating -20°C (-4°F).
SIZE: 90 x 60cm (36 x 24in).

SPECIAL FEATURES

Flowers in late spring before most other geraniums. Many of the named varieties have large flowers with rich colours and form compact clumps of foliage.

Recommended Varieties

G. sylvaticum (wood cranesbill), a beautiful plant, violet-blue with an almost white centre but pink and white forms are also found in the wild.

'Album' (AGM), white, pale foliage, comes true from seed; 'Amy Doncaster', deep blue with white eye; 'Baker's Pink', soft pink, flowers a little later than most; 'Birch Lilac', deep violet; 'Mayflower' (AGM), rich violet-blue with a white eye; f. *albiflorum* is the name given to wild white flowered variants; f. *roseum* is the name given to wild pink flowered variants; ssp. *sylvaticum* var. *wanneri*, pale rose-pink with brighter rose veins, low-growing at 30cm (12in).

Geranium sylvaticum 'Mayflower'

Geranium psilostemon

ORIGIN: North east Turkey and south west Caucasus.
SITE AND SOIL: Tolerates sun or light shade. Any good garden soil is suitable but thrives best in soils that do not dry out.
HARDINESS: Very hardy, tolerating -20°C (-4°F).
SIZE: Up to 1.2 x 1.2m (4 x 4ft).

SPECIAL FEATURES

G. psilostemon and its relatives all make large and spectacular border plants.

Geranium collinum

Recommended Varieties

G. psilostemon (syn. G. armenum) (AGM), striking bright magenta flowers with black centres and black veins, attractive foliage with autumn tints, stems need support, a vigorous plant that needs regular division; 'Bressingham Fair', a shorter form, softer in colour, a rich lilac-pink; 'Ann Folkard' (G. procurrens x G. psilostemon raised by the Rev. O G Folkard in 1973) has similar flowers to G. psilostemon but set off by golden yellow foliage, needs sun. 'Anne Thomson' (G. procurrens x G. psilostemon), an Alan Bremner, Orkney hybrid, is like 'Ann Folkard' but more compact at 55 x 90cm (22 x 36in).
'Patricia' (G. endressii x G. psilostemon), another Alan Bremner cross, is bright magenta with a dark eye, long-flowering, large leaves, height 75cm (30in).

Other species

ORIGIN: G. albiflorum is found in north and central Asia and north east Russia, G. rivulare occurs in poor alpine meadows and woods in the west and centre of the European Alps while G. collinum is a widespread species found in south east Europe, central and eastern Turkey and west and central Asia.
SITE AND SOIL: Tolerate sun or light shade. Any good garden soil is suitable but most do best in soils that do not dry out. G. collinum prefers sun and can tolerate dry sites.
HARDINESS: Very hardy, tolerating -20°C (-4°F).
SIZE: G. albiflorum and G. rivulare are 30 x 45cm (12 x 18in). G. collinum forms a loose bush up to 60cm (24in).

SPECIAL FEATURES

G. albiflorum and G. rivulare are modest plants but worth considering for the front of a border. G. collinum is unremarkable but could be useful in a wild garden where the soil is prone to drying out.

Recommended Varieties

True species only are available of: G. albiflorum, white with violet veins, purple-brown markings on leaves, stems and sepals; G. rivulare (syn. G. aconitifolium), white with violet veins; G. collinum, pink sometimes with red veins, spring foliage often tinged with yellow or pink.

Geranium psilostemon

GERANIUM PRATENSE AND RELATED TYPES

Geranium pratense, the meadow cranesbill, is seen rather less frequently these days in meadows than on verges where, in my experience, it is the commonest European species. I have seen huge stretches of roadside from the Cotswolds of England to the Tatra mountains of southern Poland almost carpeted with its glorious blue. Its relatively short flowering season mitigates against it being one of the best garden geraniums (other than in the wild garden where it is indispensable), but travel a few thousand kilometres eastwards, to find one of its relatives, and you have a garden gem in the shape of Geranium himalayense. *This is a plant I always cite as the classic example of gardeners being far too obsessed with double flowers, and the variety 'Plenum' must be grown in fifty gardens for every one that has the much more lovely single species.*

Geranium pratense

ORIGIN: Northern Europe and Asia, but has become established in other areas such as eastern North America. In England it is found most typically on chalk and limestone soils.
SITE AND SOIL: Tolerates sun or light shade and thrives in most garden soils.
HARDINESS: Very hardy, tolerating -20°C (-4°F).
SIZE: 60 x 60cm (24 x 24in) although some garden forms may attain 75-90cm (30-36in).

SPECIAL FEATURES

Easy to grow. The wild form can be grown in rough grass and is invaluable for the wild garden. Selected garden forms are good border plants for their blue flowers and attractive, if slightly floppy, clumps of foliage with good autumn tints.

Recommended Varieties

G. pratense (meadow cranesbill), violet-blue; 'Bittersweet', pale mauve-pink with paler veins, purple-tinged foliage; 'Galactic', milky white; 'Mrs Kendall Clark' (AGM), pearl-grey, flushed with soft rose, but plants sold under this name can also have violet-blue flowers with white veins, needs support; 'Plenum Caeruleum', small flowers of light lavender-blue, double; 'Plenum Violaceum' (syns. *G. p.* 'Flore Pleno', *G. p.* 'Plenum Purpureum') (AGM), small flowers of rich deep violet, double; 'Rose Queen', white with pink veins; 'Silver Queen', silver-blue but most plants on sale now are white with pale violet tinge, tall, up to 1.2m (4ft); f. *albiflorum* is the name given to wild white-flowered variants; *G. p. roseum*, mid-pink.

'Blue Cloud', pale blue, star-like flowers, finely divided foliage, 30-45 x 30-45cm (12-18 x 12-18in), is a new introduction, thought to be either a seedling from 'Nimbus' (page 21) or a *G. pratense* type.

'Brookside' (*G. pratense* x *G. clarkei* 'Kashmir Purple'), was introduced in 1989, deep clear blue, 30-45 cm (12x18 in).

'Spinners', raised by Peter Chappell of Spinners Nursery in Hampshire in the mid 1980s and introduced in 1990, is a fine plant of which the exact parentage is not known but includes *G. pratense*, purple blue, early flowering, a strong grower up to 90cm (36in).

LEFT: *Geranium pratense* 'Plenum Violaceum'

Geranium clarkei

ORIGIN: Mountains to over 4000m (1300ft) in Kashmir.
SITE AND SOIL: Tolerates sun or light shade and thrives in most garden soils.
HARDINESS: Very hardy, tolerating -20°C (-4°F).
SIZE: 30-45 x 30-45cm (12-18 x 12-18in).

SPECIAL FEATURES

Forms of G. clarkei are most suitable as clump-forming border plants, although 'Kashmir Purple' is best used as ground cover over large areas.

Recommended Varieties

G. clarkei, purple-violet or white with lilac-pink veins, finely cut foliage. The following coloured forms are commonly grown: 'Kashmir Blue' (G. pratense albiflorum x G. clarkei 'Kashmir White'), large flowers of soft pale blue, like G. pratense in size and foliage; 'Kashmir Pink', soft pink, a seedling of 'Kashmir Purple' introduced in 1990; 'Kashmir Purple', deep violet-purple with lilac-pink veins, rampant rhizomes; 'Kashmir White' (syns. G. pratense 'Rectum Album', G. rectum 'Album'), white with grey-pink veins, less vigorous than 'Kashmir Purple'. 'Nimbus' (G. collinum x G. clarkei 'Kashmir Purple'), was introduced in 1990, purple-pink with darker veins, feathery foliage tinged with yellow when young, lax habit.

Geranium himalayense

ORIGIN: As the name suggests, G. himalayense originates in the Himalayas, occurring from north east Afghanistan to central Nepal.
SITE AND SOIL: Tolerates sun or light shade and most garden soils.
HARDINESS: Very hardy, tolerating -20°C (-4°F).
SIZE: 30 x 60cm (12 x 24in).

SPECIAL FEATURES

An attractive border or ground cover plant offering beautiful flowers and dainty foliage with autumn tints, although it can be invasive. It hybridizes readily with G. pratense.

Recommended Varieties

G. himalayense (syns. G. grandiflorum, G. h. meeboldii), the largest-flowered of all Geranium species, variable, but typically a glorious, deep violet-blue that makes it, perhaps, my favourite of all geraniums; 'Gravetye' (syns. G. grandiflorum var. alpinum, G. h. alpinum) (AGM), even larger flowers with a more red centre, more compact habit; 'Irish Blue', paler blue with a larger, more red centre than 'Gravetye', very free-flowering over a long period but a vigorous plant; 'Plenum' (syn. G. h. 'Birch Double'), purplish, double, less vigorous than single flowered types and has become, in recent years, a very popular, familiar plant, although in my experience, abnormally prone to leaf-attacking insects. 'Johnson's Blue' (AGM) is a beautiful, and now famous, cross between G. himalayense and G. pratense.

Geranium 'Johnson's Blue'

Geranium himalayense

" *Nathaniel Wallich was an interesting character. Born Nathan Wolff in Denmark in 1786, he was among the first western botanists to study the extraordinarily varied and rich flora of India. And among the numerous plants named after him, the pine,* Pinus wallichianum, *the beautiful fern* Dryopteris wallichianum *and, of greater immediate concern,* Geranium wallichianum *are those I grow in my own garden. But, with due respect to the gentleman, as far as the geranium is concerned, I turn to a Welsh variant of it; if you want a geranium with a blue to match any that horticulture has to offer,* Geranium wallichianum *'Buxton's Variety' is one of the few flowers that can shame a gentian.* "

Geranium wallichianum

ORIGIN: Himalayas from north east Afghanistan to Kashmir. The popular form called 'Buxton's Variety' is named after E C Buxton of Wales in whose garden it appeared in 1920.
SITE AND SOIL: Sun or medium shade. Often said to prefer a cool, moist soil but it grows well in my garden which is fairly dry.
HARDINESS: Very hardy, tolerating -20°C (-4°F).
SIZE: 30 x 90cm (12 x 36in).

SPECIAL FEATURES

A sprawling habit that can be used for trailing over low walls, over the edges of paving or for weaving in between shrubs. The plant has a deep tap root which makes it difficult to divide so it is usually raised from seed.

Recommended Varieties
G. wallichianum, purple-pink to blue with a white centre, a variable species and it is wisest to select the glorious, named selection 'Buxton's Variety' (syn. *G. w.* 'Buxton's Blue') (AGM), spode blue flowers with white centres, and dark stamens, which become more intensely blue in autumn, comes true from seed.

Other Himalayan species

Both these species have flowers that last long into the autumn. Use their trailing habit and preference for shade in wild gardens or as ground cover.

G. lambertii (syn. *G. candicans*) makes a sprawling mound of foliage 45 x 90cm (18 x 36in). Depending on the form, the flowers are either pale pink or white with crimson veins and last well into the autumn. 'Swansdown' is a white form with a crimson centre and marbled foliage; comes true from seed.

G. procurrens was introduced in the 1840s and again in 1967 but each time it was misidentified and so wrongly named. The flowers are a dull pink-purple with a black centre. The runners die off in autumn leaving young rooted plants and although it is too vigorous for smaller gardens, it can usefully be

Geranium wallichianum

allowed to grow through hedges or grown under trees in wilder places.

'Salome' (*G. lambertii* x *G. procurrens*) is like *G. lambertii* in habit, forming a mound of foliage tinged with yellow when young. The flowers are like those of *G. procurrens* but more dramatic; a dusky pale violet-pink with darker veins and a dark centre.

Kashmir species

G. kishtvariense, introduced to the UK in 1978 following its collection by Roy Lancaster, is a bushy plant that spreads by thin underground stolons. The flowers are bright pink-purple with purple veins and it will flower until the autumn. It prefers shade or partial shade and a soil that is reasonably moist.

G. rubifolium is similar in appearance to *G. kishtvariense* but without the characteristic stolons. Its roots are intolerant of persistent wet in winter so it is likely to disappear unless given a well-drained soil in partial shade.

East Siberian species

G. dahuricum requires full sun but the other two species can tolerate both sun or partial shade. They all grow in sprawling fashion to 45-60 x 45-60cm (18-24 x 18-24in) and are suitable for the wild garden or a large rock garden.

G. erianthum, also found in Japan, Alaska and Canada (British Columbia) is a variable species, the flowers which appear from late spring to early summer ranging from pale mauve-blue with dark veins to deep purple with darker veins. The foliage is attractive and deeply-divided with good autumn colour.

G. wlassovianum is also found in Mongolia and northern China in damp areas but grows well in drier conditions in gardens. The flowers are dusky magenta-purple or sometimes pink with veins. It forms a clump of hairy foliage which is tinged pink-bronze in spring.

G. dahuricum is also found in Mongolia and east across northern China to the Pacific. The flowers are pale pink with red veins and although not spectacular, it makes a useful gap filler as it is long-flowering. The new foliage is tinged pink and yellow.

Chinese species

Both species come from south west China and can reach up to 60cm (24in) in height. They have unusual flowers that need to be appreciated at close quarters and so are best grown in a raised bed, in partial shade.

G. pogonanthum which also occurs in Burma where Kingdon Ward found it, has dusky pink flowers like miniature cyclamen, needs replanting when roots work their way above soil, and foliage marbled with yellowish green.

G. sinense (syns. *G. delavayi*, *G. platypetalum*), flowers are like *G. phaeum* (page 42), dark maroon almost black, pink at the base, and particularly attractive to hoverflies.

'Pagoda' (*G. sinense* x *G. yunnanense*), a Bremner hybrid, has unusually-coloured flowers of dark red-purple, mottled foliage, a loose habit, growing to about 60 cm (24 in), and is useful for wild or woodland areas with dry soils.

European species

G. palustre is found naturally in damp areas in east and central Europe although it can tolerate dryness in gardens. Its flowers are a rather harsh bright magenta-pink with dark purple veins. It is long-flowering so can be used as a gap filler in borders, although it self seeds and will therefore spread.

Geranium kishtvariense

Geranium procurrens

SOME ALPINE GERANIUMS

❝ *The plants that I have included here evoke some of the greatest names in the history of botanical exploration and conjure up the years when plants from the rich storehouse of China were pouring to the West. These three species passed through the hands of Ernest Wilson, William Purdom, Reginald Farrer and the Veitch nursery on their way to European gardens. Geranium farreri was found by the great Yorkshireman at 3,600m (1200ft) on the Red Ridge of the Min-Shan in Western Gansu, China and later named in his honour by the Austrian born botanist Dr Otto Stapf of Kew. Peter Yeo describes it as the most charming of all alpine species of geranium and, like me, finds Farrer's own words* 'irresistibly quotable'. *Writing in one of the plant exploration classics, his* On The Eaves Of The World, *Farrer said 'all the wide wilderness of shingle and scree was tufted with this new treasure. . . a crowded dance of its faintly flushing blossoms, silvery in the cold air of that day'. Who could read words like that and not want to rush to the nearest plant catalogue and order it?* ❞

Geranium farreri (syn. G. napuligerum)

ORIGIN: West China, where it was found by Reginald Farrer just before the First World War.
SITE AND SOIL: Best grown in a pot in an alpine house, or could be tried on a rock garden or scree with very good drainage.
HARDINESS: Very hardy, tolerating -20°C (-4°F).
SIZE: 10-15cm (4-6in).

SPECIAL FEATURES

A delightful alpine *Geranium* with pale pink flowers and blue black anthers in late spring. It disappears in winter.

BELOW: *Geranium farreri*
OPPOSITE TOP: *Geranium orientalitibeticum*
OPPOSITE BOTTOM: *Geranium pylzowianum*

Geranium orientalitibeticum (syn. *G. stapfianum* var. *roseum*)

ORIGIN: South west China where it grows in scrub at 2,300-2,88 m. Introduced into cultivation by the Veitch nursery, and possibly among Ernest Wilson's collections in 1903.
SITE AND SOIL: Sunny site preferred.
HARDINESS: Very hardy, tolerating -20°C (-4°F).
SIZE: 20-40cm (8-16in).

SPECIAL FEATURES

The flowers are deep pink with a white central zone and the beautiful foliage is marbled with yellow. I feel confident in describing this as my most-loved foliage *Geranium*. Its neat clumps are admired every year in my own garden and its potential for being more widely grown is surely only limited by the problem that people have with its name. It spreads by underground tubers, so can swamp other alpines on a rock garden. Grow it, as I do, as a border edging, between paving or in a container.

Geranium pylzowianum

ORIGIN: West China where it is found in alpine pastures, meadows and rock ledges at 2,400-4,250m (7,900-14,000ft). It was collected by William Purdom in 1910, and like *G. orientalitibeticum*, introduced into cultivation by Veitch.
SITE AND SOIL: In the wild requires scree conditions so in gardens should be given a free-draining soil in full sun.
HARDINESS: Very hardy, tolerating -20°C (-4°F).
SIZE: 12-25cm (5-10in) high.

SPECIAL FEATURES

It flowers in late spring or early summer then becomes dormant until the following spring. The flowers are large in relation to the size of the plant and are a deep rose pink with darker veins and a green centre. Underground runners and tiny tubers make it easy to establish, if invasive, but because it is dormant apart from the spring this does not usually present a problem.

GERANIUM SANGUINEUM

" *In Britain,* Geranium sanguineum *is what botanists call an 'indicator' plant. It is one of a group of ten or more native species that also includes* Plantago media, Campanula glomerata *and* Viola hirta. *If several of this group are found growing naturally together, it is almost certain that the soil has a high content of calcium carbonate and is therefore strongly alkaline. I know of very few places where* G. sanguineum, *the bloody cranesbill, grows naturally that are not on chalk or limestone. This is one of life's curious facts because in gardens it will grow happily on soils that are certainly on the acid side of neutral, although very acidic conditions do not suit it. In the wild, it tends to be described as 'locally common', although I think it has become more frequent in recent years. It certainly isn't a plant that conceals itself and if it is present, you will see its patches of blood-red coloured flowers shouting out from high up on limestone cliffs when the plant itself is barely visible. Although this colour is almost too assertive in gardens, there are subtler shades selected from it, as well as the white variant that is almost ubiquitous among geraniums, and overall, it is a plant to have in every geranium collection.* "

ORIGIN: Occurs in most of Europe, the Caucasus and also northern Turkey in dry scrub areas. In Britain it is generally found on mountains, coastal rocks and sea cliffs.

SITE AND SOIL: Best in sun but can tolerate partial shade. Tolerates most soils but prefers well-drained conditions.

HARDINESS: Very hardy, tolerating -20°C (-4°F).

SIZE: 30 x 45cm (12 x 18in) but compact forms are only 15-20 x 30cm (6-8 x 12in).

SPECIAL FEATURES

Low mats of deeply divided leaves with good autumn colour. Flowers in early summer, a rather harsh colour in the true species but garden forms offer a wide range of shades of pink or white. Ideal for dry, sunny spots such as rock gardens, paving, or at the front of a raised bed or border. Paler shades blend particularly well with old rose varieties.

Geranium sanguineum **'Album'**

Recommended Varieties

G. sanguineum (bloody cranesbill), typically purple-red, but a variable species; 'Album' (AGM), white, an open habit up to 60 cm (24 in) across; 'Cedric Morris', discovered by Sir Cedric Morris on the Gower coast in South Wales, magenta-pink, larger flowers and leaves than most forms; 'Elsbeth', a recent introduction with large, bright purple flowers; 'Glenluce', found on a cliff near Glenluce, Scotland by A T Johnson in the 1930s, clear pink; 'John Elsley', bright pink with darker veins, a recent introduction from the USA, compact; 'Max Frei', magenta, good autumn colour, a German introduction with neat habit, compact; 'Nanum', rose-red, compact; 'Nyewood', similar to 'Max Frei'; 'Shepherd's Warning' (AGM), arguably the finest and most famous of all of the variants, and was raised from var. *striatum* by the celebrated alpine nurseryman Jack Drake at his nursery at Aviemore, Scotland, deep magenta pink, compact; var. *striatum* (syns. *G. sanguineum.* var. *lancastrense*, *G. sanguineum.* var. *prostratum*) (AGM), from which 'Shepherd's Warning' was raised, is pale pink with crimson veins, begins flowering in late spring, native to Walney Island off the coast of Cumbria, variable in habit but, significantly and valuably, always dwarf; var. *striatum* 'Splendens' pale pink with crimson veins, a later-flowering variety. 'Dilys' (*G. sanguineum* x *G. procurrens*), is an Alan Bremner hybrid, soft purple with darker veins, forms a mound 23 x 90cm (9 x 36in), with the foliage of *G. sanguineum* and the long flowering period of *G. procurrens*. 'Diva' (*G. sanguineum* x *G. swatense*), another of Bremner's crosses, is purple-pink, golden foliage, branching stems to 45cm (18in).

Geranium sanguineum 'Shepherd's Warning'

Geranium sanguineum

SOME SOUTHERN HEMISPHERE GERANIUMS

" *Although South Africa is the homeland of the genus* Pelargonium, *it also yields some attractive and rather unusual* Geranium *species. And as evidence of the global distribution of these plants, there are also interesting examples from New Zealand. Remembering that pelargoniums are not hardy in northern temperate climates, it might be thought that these geraniums too are of value only as summer plants but, with care, some will survive over the winter outdoors. Others are useful when they can be taken under cover in winter while some have proved valuable as the parents of hybrids with hardier species. None justify being neglected.* "

Geranium sessiliflorum

ORIGIN: *Geranium sessiliflorum* has three subspecies, of which the New Zealand native *G. s.* ssp. *novae-zelandiae* is the best known and most widely cultivated. The others are ssp. *sessiliflorum* from South America and ssp. *brevicaule* 'Glabrum Group' from Tasmania and the south east highlands of Australia.
SITE AND SOIL: Needs a sunny site and a well-drained soil or gritty compost.
HARDINESS: Moderately hardy, tolerating -10°C to -15°C (14°F to -4°F)
SIZE: 8-10 x 20cm (3-4 x 8in).

SPECIAL FEATURES

A neat carpet-like plant for a rock garden or between paving, offering summer flowers. Some forms have interesting foliage colours.

Recommended Varieties

G. sessiliflorum ssp. *novae-zelandiae*, white, the flowers often hidden among the green foliage; 'Nigricans', a dark-leaved form, the leaves unfold to a bronze colour and then turn orange as they age. 'Sea Fire' (*G. sessiliflorum* 'Nigricans' x *G. x oxonianum*), a Bremner, Orkney hybrid, is bright red pink with pale eye, a long-flowering, low spreading evergreen plant, 20 x 45cm (8 x 18in) for rock garden or front of the border. 'Sea Pink' (*G. sessiliflorum* 'Nigrescens x *G. x oxonianum*), pink, bronze-tinted foliage, has a similar habit and comes from the same nursery. 'Stanhoe' (*G. sessiliflorum* x *G. traversii*) is the result of a cross that occurred in a garden in Norfolk, pink, with a similar habit to *G. traversii*, needs full sun, for rock garden or alpine trough.

Geranium sessiliflorum

Geranium traversii var. elegans

ORIGIN From the Chatham Islands (650 km east of New Zealand) where it grows naturally on sea cliffs. When *G. traversii* was first discovered in the 19th century and subsequently named by Sir Joseph Hooker, it was described as having white flowers and as recently as 1946, this form still occurred, at least in gardens. However, it is now thought to be extinct, leaving only the pink-flowered *G. traversii* var. *elegans*.
SITE AND SOIL Needs a sunny site and a well-drained soil or gritty compost.
HARDINESS Moderately hardy, tolerating -10°C to -15°C (14°F to -4°F)
SIZE 15-20cm (6-8in), mound forming.

SPECIAL FEATURES

Ideal for providing summer to autumn flowers on a sunny rock garden, scree or trough. Easily lost in winter, probably, as with many such plants, due to wet, so either offer protection by cloches, grow it in an alpine house, or propagate it annually by seeds or cuttings.

Geranium traversii

Recommended Varieties

G. traversii var.*elegans*, shell pink, hairy, grey-green foliage; *G. s.* ssp. *novae-zelandiae* 'Nigricans' x *G. traversii* var. *elegans* is a pretty, though unnamed, hybrid, similar to *G. traversii* var.*elegans* but less hairy and with white flowers flushed with rose. 'Joy' (*G. traversii* var. *elegans* x *G. lambertii*), one of A Bremner's Orkney hybrids, is soft pink with darker veins, long-flowering, almost evergreen, suitable for rock garden or front of the border.

'Seaspray' (*G. traversii* var.*elegans* x *G. sessiliflorum* 'Nigricans') is another hybrid raised by Alan Bremner on Orkney and recently introduced. The flowers are pale pink to white and are produced through the summer. It has bronze foliage that forms a mound 100cm (40in) across. 'Orkney Pink', from the same source, is a more complex cross ((*G. traversii* x *G. sessiliflorum* 'Nigricans') x *G. x oxonianum*), bright purple-pink, bronze foliage, long-flowering, low-growing to 15cm (6in), dies down

after frost, needs sun. A plant called 'Pink Spice' has been heavily promoted in British garden centres recently and said to be a 'new evergreen form from the south island of New Zealand'. Its main feature is its bronze foliage, with small bright pink flowers that appear intermittently from spring to autumn. Its size is described as 15 x 90cm (6 x 36in), and it tends to begin as a low-growing plant with tiny leaves but the later leaves are larger and it forms a dome 30-45 x 30-45cm (12-18 x 12-18in).

South African species

ORIGIN: *G. incanum* is found over an area stretching from Hout Bay to Port Alfred in the extreme South-east and it is a common roadside plant in the southern Cape; the clo-sely related *G. magniflorum* originates from Drakensberg in southern Natal.
SITE AND SOIL: Need a sunny, sheltered site and a well-drained soil or gritty compost.
HARDINESS: Fairly hardy, tolerating -5°C to -10°C (23°F to 14°F).
SIZE: 20-23cm (8-9in).

SPECIAL FEATURES

These are showy little plants, offering summer flowers and pretty foliage. Best grown in a trough, raised bed or in a sunny rock garden. Not reliable in severe winters but can readily be propagated by seeds or cuttings.

Recommended Varieties

G. incanum var. *multifidum*, (the form most commonly grown in Britain), often sold simply under the name *G. incanum*) is red-purple with darker veins, the foliage is green above, silver beneath, with a parsley-like aroma when crushed, autumn tints; *G. magniflorum* is plum-purple with darker veins and a white base.

Geranium incanum

SOME NORTH AMERICAN GERANIUMS

" *North America does not have the same importance as Europe and Asia in the geranium world. There are fewer species overall, a number of those that do occur are either introduced and naturalized or have more significant centres of natural occurrence elsewhere, and also,* *North American geraniums are less important as garden plants. But that does not mean they should be ignored. In a shady part of my own garden I have a most attractive pink flowered species, as yet unidentified, grown from seed I collected from a forest in the Rocky Mountains of* *British Columbia. Indeed, with one exception, the species that I recommend here are from the western side of the continent but to confound those who think of* Geranium *as a genus of cool-temperate climates, at least two occur as far south as Arizona and New Mexico.* "

Geranium maculatum

ORIGIN: Eastern North America as far west as Manitoba and Kansas in fields, meadows and open woodland.
SITE AND SOIL: A sunny, or partially shady site in moist or wet soil is preferred and, as in the wild, it will readily naturalize near streams.
HARDINESS: Very hardy, tolerating -20°C (-4°F).
SIZE: 60 x 45cm (24 x 18in).

SPECIAL FEATURES

Spring flowers with handsome foliage that can be used to good effect to begin the season in a border, bog garden or wild area. The root is tuberous, almost woody.

Recommended Varieties
The true species G. maculatum is pale to deep pink with a white centre, large, divided foliage, will self-seed; f. albiflorum is a white form.

Geranium oreganum

ORIGIN: Western United States, from southern Washington and Oregon, as far south as northern California.
SITE AND SOIL: Fairly moist, moderately rich soil such as a herbaceous or mixed border.
HARDINESS: Very hardy, tolerating -20°C (-4°F).
SIZE: 60 x 120cm (24 x 48in).

SPECIAL FEATURES

Abundant large flowers of deep rose-pink in mid summer, and foliage rather like that of G. pratense. Use its spreading habit by allowing it to weave between other border plants, shrubs or ornamental grasses.

ABOVE: *Geranium maculatum f. albiflorum*   **RIGHT:** *Geranium oreganum*

Geranium fremontii

ORIGIN: Western United States from Wyoming as far south as New Mexico and Arizona.
SITE AND SOIL: Requires a sunny position in a well-drained to fairly dry soil.
HARDINESS: Very hardy, tolerating -20°C (-4°F).
SIZE: 60 x 120cm (24 x 48in).

SPECIAL FEATURES

Large, attractive flowers of rose-pink on flopping stems. Ideally grown in a informal border or cottage garden. The thick rootstocks need to be replanted when the roots have worked their way above the soil. The plants are covered in sticky hairs and have a distinctly unpleasant scent.

Geranium viscosissimum

ORIGIN: Western North America from British Columbia and Alberta to northern California and South Dakota. Found naturally in meadows and woodlands.
SITE AND SOIL: Will tolerate both sun or partial shade, and most soils.
HARDINESS: Hardy, tolerating -15°C to -20°C (5°F to -4°F).
SIZE: 20 to 30cm (18-36in).

SPECIAL FEATURES

Flower colour varies from almost white through pale to purple-pink to rich

Geranium fremontii

fuchsia red with darker veins and sometimes a white centre. Like *G. fremontii*, this is another sticky, strongly smelling species and, similarly, the thick rootstocks should be replanted when the roots have worked their way above the soil. In the wild, of course, the plants simply become untidy.

Geranium richardsonii

ORIGIN: Western North America from British Columbia and Saskatchewan south to California, South Dakota and New Mexico.
SITE AND SOIL: Thrives best in sun and moist soil.
HARDINESS: Very hardy, tolerating at least -20°C (-4°F).
SIZE: 30-60cm (12-24in).

SPECIAL FEATURES

Worth trying beside water or in a moist border for spring flowers. A variable species (the flowers can be white or tinged with pink, often with purple veins), so try to buy plants when in flower, bright green glossy foliage. The thick rootstocks should be replanted when the roots have worked their way above the soil.

GERANIUM ASPHODELOIDES

" *The Dissecta Section of the genus* Geranium *is well known to many gardeners though without most of them realising it because there are two* Geranium *species that attain significance in Britain and elsewhere in Europe as garden weeds.* Geranium robertianum *(page 45) is one, and* Geranium dissectum, *which is placed in this part of the genus, is the other. Fortunately, they are rarely serious weeds, but nor are they are of great value as garden plants. However the Dissecta Section does include another species that I always consider among the under-appreciated garden geraniums. I first came across* Geranium asphodeloides *many years ago in a garden in the East of England where the white form was carpeting part of a very well designed rock garden. It now does the same in mine and is, I believe, a species that deserves to be much more widely grown.* "

SPECIAL FEATURES

Flowers throughout the summer, and except in severe winters, the fresh green leaves are almost evergreen. Very attractive when allowed to cascade over raised beds or spread out at the front of a border. Self-seeds freely in most gardens but not deeply rooted and therefore easily kept in check.

Geranium asphodeloides

ORIGIN: Southern Europe, Lebanon and Syria to northern Turkey depending on the subspecies.
SITE AND SOIL: Thrives in full sun but can be grown in light shade. Most garden soils are suitable.
HARDINESS: Moderately hardy, tolerating -10°C to -15°C (14°F to 4°F).
SIZE: Varies from 20-30 x 45-60cm (8-12 x 18-24in).

Geranium asphodeloides 'Starlight'

Recommended Varieties

G. asphodeloides is a variable species: ssp. *asphodeloides*, from much of southern Europe, flowers can be white, pale pink or deep pink with darker veins, narrow petals give the flowers a star-like appearance; ssp. *crenophilum*, from Lebanon and Syria, deep rose pink with darker veins, quite reliably evergreen; ssp. *sintenisii* from northern Turkey, pale pink or purple and very free-flowering, is covered with red hairs which make a striking winter feature, should be replanted when roots form above ground.

Two named varieties were introduced in 1990, both are early to flower and continue to bloom for a long period: 'Prince Regent', pale lilac with darker veins, and 'Starlight', white.

" *The tuberous geraniums form an interesting and distinct group. All occur in places with very hot, dry summers; places with a classically Mediterranean style of climate, typified by the Mediterranean region itself. Their behaviour, and the form of their rootstock, are intriguing adaptations to these conditions. The roots are swollen to form a storage organ, a tuber, which generally grows horizontally, and the individual tubers are joined together by thin lengths of rhizome. There is nothing else quite like it in the genus. And because of the summer drought of their homelands, the plants typically flower in early summer and then become dormant, disappearing from view until the following spring; among those I recommend here, the only exception is* Geranium malviflorum *which sometimes produces new leaves in autumn. These unusual bits of botany have a bearing on the way the plants should be used in gardens. In my own garden, they are among the earliest geraniums to flower and I therefore plan their positioning with the spring, rather than the summer, garden flora in mind.* "

Geranium macrostylum

ORIGIN: Greece, Albania, the southern part of former Yugoslavia and central and south western Turkey.
SITE AND SOIL: Full sun in a relatively poor soil or gritty compost.
HARDINESS: Hardy, tolerating -15°C to -20°C (5°F to -4°F).
SIZE: 38cm (15in) high.

SPECIAL FEATURES

Late spring flowers, best grown in containers or between paving. The flowers are pale pink with a darker base. This is an attractive, moderately hairy plant that will readily become established through the rather small, easily dispersed tubers and can be invasive. Because of this, it shouldn't be planted where it can't easily be weeded out.

Geranium malviflorum (syn. G. atlanticum)

ORIGIN: Southern Spain, Morocco and Algeria.
SITE AND SOIL: A sunny, well-drained spot, drought tolerant.
HARDINESS: Fairly hardy, tolerating -5°C to -10°C (23°F to 14°F).
SIZE: Up to 45 x 45cm (18 x 18in).

SPECIAL FEATURES

This has the largest leaves of any of the tuberous geraniums and in some forms they arise in autumn to persist throughout the winter; in others, they are not produced until spring. This is a fine and imposing plant with superb lilac-blue flowers in spring (supposedly like those of a *Malva*).

Geranium tuberosum

ORIGIN: The Mediterranean region as far east as western Iran and is of-ten found as a weed in cornfields and vineyards. This is the longest-cultivated tuberous geraniums, having been grown in gardenssince1885.
SITE AND SOIL: Sunny, well-drained sites.
HARDINESS: Moderately hardy, tolerating -10°C to -15°C (14°F to 4°F).
SIZE: 20-25cm (8-10in) high.

SPECIAL FEATURES

Flowers are purple-rose with darker veins, the foliage is feathery. Similar to *G. macrostylum* but not as hairy, and with larger flowers. An ideal plant for the larger rock garden.

Geranium tuberosum

GERANIUM IBERICUM AND RELATED TYPES

❝ Geranium ibericum *is a Caucasian species of merit – enough for it to have been grown in British gardens as long ago as 1802 which makes it one of the longest-cultivated geraniums. It is a warm-climate plant which may partly explain why it has never become naturalised in Britain over these past two centuries, although it has established itself in north-west France.* Geranium ibericum *is certainly a good garden plant, and it has been successful in the recent series of warm, drier British summers. But alone, it would never have entered geranium-growing folklore. For that, it can thank its close Caucasian relative,* Geranium platypetalum *because somewhere, at sometime, the two hybridized. Their offspring so impressed the Swedish botanist Dr Nils Hylander that he accorded it almost the ultimate compliment when he named, it in 1961,* Geranium x magnificum. *Despite having so recently been named,* Geranium x magnificum *has been with us for a considerable time. It certainly arose before 1871 because there is a herbarium specimen in existence of that date which is clearly the same hybrid. For years this, and other specimens, had been incorrectly called* Geranium platypetalum *and even today, when you try to buy plants of* Geranium x magnificum, *they are often given the names of one of the parent plants. I have been told that it is the commonest geranium in British gardens but, although popular, I find it hard to believe it is that popular.* ❞

Geranium ibericum

ORIGIN: North east Turkey, Caucasus. The familiar and popular hybrid G. x magnificum has been grown in gardens for over a hundred years but where the initial cross was made is not known.

SITE AND SOIL: Sun or light shade preferred. Tolerant of most soils including relatively dry sites.

HARDINESS: Very hardy, tolerating -20°C (-4°F).

SIZE: 45-60 x 60cm (18-24 x 24in).

SPECIAL FEATURES

Attractive border plants and good choices for underplanting roses although unfortunately, the flowering period is brief. Soft pink roses blend beautifully with both G. ibericum and its relatives.

Geranium ibericum

Recommended Varieties and Related Varieties:

G. ibericum, violet-blue with purple veins, a hairy plant with deeply divided foliage; G. i. ssp. jubatum is very similar; G. platypetalum (syn. G. ibericum var. platypetalum), deep violet-blue, paler at the centre and with darker veins, similar to G. ibericum but the foliage has broader lobes; G. x magnificum (syn. G. ibericum var. platypetalum) (AGM), violet-blue with darker veins, free-flowering, attractive foliage with autumn tints, a sterile hybrid of G. ibericum and G. platypetalum, a better though smaller (30-45 x 45cm (12-18 x 18in)) garden plant than either parent, but a confusing plant to buy because the various clones available are often labelled with the name of the parents.

Geranium x magnificum

Geranium gracile

Geranium gracile

ORIGIN: North eastern Turkey, southern Caucasus and northern Iran, grows naturally in woodlands.
SITE AND SOIL: Moist, preferably slightly rich soil and light shade.
HARDINESS: Hardy, tolerating -15°C to -20°C (5°F to -4°F).
SIZE: 40 x 40cm (16 x 16in).

SPECIAL FEATURES

Summer flowering. Distinctive eyelash-like markings on pink petals with a white base. The flowers are variable however, so when buying, look for plants with well-developed markings. The entire plant is conspicuously and distinctively hairy; it has been described as a hairy version of *Geranium nodosum* (page 14).

Geranium libani

ORIGIN: Lebanon, west Syria and central and south Turkey.
SITE AND SOIL: Best in a sunny well-drained spot.
HARDINESS: Moderately hardy, tolerates -10°C to -15°C (14°F to -4°F).
SIZE: 40cm (15in).

SPECIAL FEATURES

A spring-flowering rock plant that becomes dormant over the summer, with the glossy leaves appearing again in the autumn. The flowers are violet-blue or violet.

GERANIUM RENARDII

❝ *I do not know what it is about the mountains of the Caucasus that have caused them to be such a fount of valuable plants, but for species as different as apples and campanulas, they have provided much that we grow and admire today. Intriguingly, it is also one of the most ethnically diverse regions for human populations too. And as is apparent from my descriptions of* Geranium *species, a good number of these also originated in this wild region, wedged between Europe and Asia.* Geranium renardii *is another of them, and it is a species that exemplifies the attraction that some of the genus have for alpine enthusiasts. The alpine expert Walter Ingwersen, whose nursery still bears his name, found it in the wild and introduced it into cultivation. It is a striking and distinctive species and I am baffled that Ingwersen's nursery no longer lists it. The species was granted an AGM but has more recently received a new lease of life through the work of the hybridist Alan Bremner in Orkney who has crossed* Geranium renardii *with other species to produce attractive variants for the modern alpine garden.* **❞**

SPECIAL FEATURES

Neat clumps of characteristic, very sparsely-divided foliage. The leaves are a soft sage green with a velvet texture. Ideally grown in a rock garden, on a paved terrace, between paving or at the front of a border. The summer flowering period is brief but the foliage offers constant interest.

ORIGIN Caucasus. Found by the distinguished alpine nurseryman, Walter Ingwersen of Sussex growing on rock cliffs. It was introduced into cultivation in 1935.

SITE AND SOIL Sun or partial shade; to encourage flowering, the plant should be grown in full sun and in a fairly dry soil, low in nutrients. This a classic example of the value of knowing the conditions in which a plant occurs naturally in order to succeed best with its cultivation.

HARDINESS Very hardy, tolerating -20°C (-4°F).

SIZE 20-30 x 20-30cm (8-12 x 8-12in).

Recommended Varieties

G. renardii (AGM), white with violet veins, wrinkled, soft green foliage; 'Whiteknights' (syn. *G. r.* blue), lilac-blue; 'Zetterland' ('Zetterlund'), purple-blue with darker veins, a looser habit than the species. 'Chantilly' (*G. renardii* x *G. gracile*), is an Alan Bremner cross, lavender pink, similar to *G. gracile* but more compact at 45cm (18in), it has leaves the shape of *G. renardii* but they are light green. 'Philippe Vapelle' (*G. renardii* x *G. platypetalum*), another Bremner cross, has large flowers of bluish purple with darker veins, free-flowering, foliage like *G. renardii* but dark grey-green.

Geranium renardii

Geranium pyrenaicum

ORIGIN: South western and western Europe, east to the Caucasus. Introduced to more northerly localities and naturalised in the south and east of England, where it grows in fields, beside roads and on waste ground.
SITE AND SOIL: Will grow in a range of conditions, tolerating medium shade and most types of soil.
HARDINESS: Very hardy, tolerating -20°C (-4°F).
SIZE: 30 x 30cm (12 x 12in)

SPECIAL FEATURES

Evergreen mounds of aromatic foliage. Long-flowering, from late spring to autumn. It is a prolific self-seeder so is best restricted to a wild garden or woodland area.

Recommended Varieties

G. pyrenaicum, purple-pink, sometimes white, long-flowering, rounded foliage, evergreen; 'Bill Wallis', purple; f. *albiflorum*, a white form, although in cool weather it is tinged with pink.

Geranium albanum

ORIGIN: South east Caucasus and part of Iran, where it grows among shrubby vegetation.
SITE AND SOIL: Will grow in most positions and soils.
HARDINESS: Very hardy, tolerating -20°C (-4°F).
SIZE: 30-45 x 30-45cm (12-18 x 12-18in)

SPECIAL FEATURES

A reliable, summer-flowering species, it can scramble up shrubs so is worth considering to extend the season of interest in a spring-flowering shrub border. As a semi-evergreen, it is suitable as a ground cover plant or for a wild garden. The flowers are bright pink with magenta veins.

RIGHT: *Geranium albanum*

Geranium polyanthes

ORIGIN: Himalayas from Nepal to south west China where its natural habitat is in alpine meadows.
SITE AND SOIL: A sunny site and moist but well-drained soil.
HARDINESS: Very hardy, tolerating -20°C (-4°F).
SIZE: 20-40cm (8-16in).

SPECIAL FEATURES

An attractive plant for the rock garden or front of the border with deep pink flowers and slightly succulent foliage. It tends to be late coming into growth, often not until late spring and then blooms in mid-summer. The roots are red-brown, thick and knobbly and should be replanted if they work up above soil level. *Geranium polyanthes* can be difficult to grow and short-lived, tending to die out after a few years, though it is easy to propagate.

Geranium pyrenaicum **'Bill Wallis'**

GERANIUM MACRORRHIZUM AND OTHER

" There is a rather dry, fairly shaded border on the north side of my house. It faces north-east, not the most favourable location for growing plants of any type. But it is also rather prominent, being passed by every visitor to my front door. Geranium macrorrhizum grows there, and apparently relishes the conditions. And it also manages to provide changing interest because there are more varieties of this one ground-covering plant than of ten or more other geranium species. "

Geranium macrorrhizum

ORIGIN: From the mountains of southern Europe especially the south side of the Alps and eastwards to the Carpathians, but it has become naturalised in other parts of Europe too, including, to a limited extent, southern England. Its typical habitat would be in partial shade among rocks, scrub and in woodland. This is a variable species that has often been introduced from the wild, not only as an ornamental plant but also for perfumery and tanning.

SITE AND SOIL: A very tolerant and valuable species that can grow in dry shade but also thrives in sun and other situations.

HARDINESS: Very hardy, tolerating -20°C (-4°F).

SIZE: 30 x 60cm (12 x 24in), although many of the newer introductions are lower growing at only 15cm (6in) high.

SPECIAL FEATURES

Reliable, weed-suppressing ground cover plant with slightly sticky, aromatic leaves. The foliage is semi-evergreen but with attractive red autumn tints. The species is valuable in gardens for planting in difficult areas such as dry shade, although for more striking flowers look for a named variety. Many of these are also good border plants, flowering in early summer and again in autumn.

Geranium macrorrhizum

Recommended Varieties

G. macrorrhizum (syn. *G. m. roseum*), pink to purple or white, light green foliage; 'Album' (AGM), white with pink stamens and calyces, introduced from the mountains of Bulgaria by Walter Ingwersen; 'Bevan's Variety', deep magenta with red sepals, a very striking plant with exceptionally bold colour, not easy to blend with anything else; 'Czakor', deep magenta-pink; 'Ingwersen's Variety' (AGM), soft rose-pink, pale green, slightly glossy foliage, a superb plant and another introduction by Walter Ingwersen, found in Montenegro in 1929; 'Lohfelden', pale pink almost white with deeper pink veins, a recent German introduction, low-growing; 'Pindus', red-purple, a recent introduction, low-growing; 'Ridsko', magenta-pink, a recent introduction, deciduous and low-growing; 'Spessart', two forms are sold under this name, one with white flowers is similar to *G. m.* 'Album', the other has pink flowers.

Geranium dalmaticum

ORIGIN: South western part of former Yugoslavia and Albania. It was introduced into cultivation by Walter Ingwersen in 1947. 'Album' is thought to have arisen in cultivation and was first shown by Blooms Nurseries in 1956. The related *G. cataractarum* comes from southern Spain and Morocco, where it grows on damp or shady limestone rocks.

SITE AND SOIL: Sun or partial shade, but if growing in northern Britain, give it full sun to ensure plenty of flowers. Any good garden soil is suitable.

HARDINESS: Very hardy, tolerating -20°C (-4°F).

SIZE: Forms a neat cushion 10-15cm (4-6in) high. *G. cataractarum* is 15cm (6in) or so high when confined in a container but in moist shade it should reach twice that height.

SPECIAL FEATURES

Dwarf plants for summer colour in a trough, between paving or in a small rock garden. Easy to grow and propagate (take root cuttings of *G. dalmaticum* and stem cuttings of *G. cataractarum*).

Recommended Varieties and Related Species:

G. dalmaticum (AGM), shell pink or white, glossy aromatic foliage with autumn tints; 'Album', white, slightly tinged with pink, less vigorous than the species; *G. cataractarum*, bright pink with orange-red anthers, evergreen foliage resembling the common native species *G. robertianum* but paler, short-lived.

Geranium dalmaticum

Geranium x cantabrigiense

Geranium x cantabrigiense

ORIGIN: A sterile hybrid between *G. macrorrhizum* and *G. dalmaticum*. The hybrid has arisen several times but a deliberate cross was made in 1974 by Dr Helen Keifer at Cambridge and named in 1985 by Dr Peter Yeo, the distinguished authority on the genus *Geranium*.
SITE AND SOIL: Sun or medium shade, will grow in most garden soils.
HARDINESS: Very hardy, tolerating -20°C (-4°F).
SIZE: 23 x 30cm (9 x 12in).

SPECIAL FEATURES

Excellent low-growing ground cover. Spreads, but never aggressively, and is easily contained. Aromatic evergreen foliage with good autumn colour.

Recommended Varieties

G. x cantabrigiense (syn. *G. dalmaticum x macrorrhizum*), 'Biokovo', white tinged with pink at the base and a less dense habit; this form has become very popular and was named after the mountains in Bosnia where it was discovered by the German nurseryman Hans Simon; 'Cambridge', rose-mauve; 'Karmina', deep pink, a German hybrid; 'Saint Ola', large white flowers with overlapping petals, a recent introduction raised by Alan Bremner in Orkney.

GERANIUM CINEREUM AND RELATED TYPES

" Apart from the rather infrequently used, though perfectly legitimate English name 'cranesbill', almost no Geranium *is ever referred to by gardeners other than by its Latin name. And yet I doubt if any of those other Latin names has passed as readily into the currency of everyday gardening language as* Geranium cinereum. *In large measure, this is due to one rather special variety, for in hearing myself say* Geranium cinereum, *I can hear another ten voices adding 'Ballerina'. The words are almost inseparable. It is a wonderful plant, and an interesting one too, for it is not a selection but a hybrid, although not one between two different species. 'Ballerina' is unusual because it is a hybrid of two subspecies of* Geranium cinereum. *The cross was made at the well-known nursery of Blooms at Bressingham, England and its popularity and familiarity must be due in large measure to the business acumen of a large commercial enterprise. Had 'Ballerina' arisen at a small, less promotion-conscious concern, it might today be a little-known rarity. One of the merits of 'Ballerina', something seen in a few other hybrid geraniums like* Geranium x magnificum *(page 34), is that the flowering season is very long, brought about largely because the hybrid is sterile – it does not set seed, a process that almost inevitably leads to flowering coming to an end. "*

Geranium cinereum 'Ballerina'

ORIGIN: Central Pyrenees. *G. cinereum* is variable and has been split into subspecies which may merit being regarded as separate species. The related *G. argenteum* is from the French Alps, Italy and former Yugoslavia and the two hybridise readily, the hybrid being given the name *G. x lindavicum*.

SITE AND SOIL: These are low-growing, often mat-forming plants of typically alpine habit and require a well-drained soil or a gritty compost, low in nutrients, especially nitrogen, to promote flowering. Plant in an open, sunny site or grow in an alpine house.

HARDINESS: Very hardy, tolerating -20°C (-4°F) but you may need to protect outdoor plants from winter wet by placing a small glass cloche over them.

SIZE: 15cm (6in), rosette habit.

SPECIAL FEATURES

Silver or grey-green foliage bearing well-spaced and often very brightly coloured flowers. Best displayed in a pot, trough, rock garden or scree.

Recommended varieties and similar species:

G. cinereum, pale pink with darker veins, a variable species among which the best forms are: 'Ballerina' (AGM), a hybrid between *G. cinereum* subsp. *cinereum* and *G. cinereum* subsp. *subcaulescens*, purple-pink with darker veins and centre, forming a wide mat, arguably the best plant ever raised or introduced by Blooms Nurseries of Norfolk; 'Lawrence Flatman', another Blooms introduction and named after their plant breeder, is similar to 'Ballerina' but more vigorous and with the petals having a dark mark towards the apex; *G. c.* subsp. *subcaulescens* (AGM), brilliant crimson-magenta, darker foliage with darker veins and black centre, one of the brightest coloured of all geraniums; 'Giuseppii', less brash colour than the type with a much less distinct black centre; 'Splendens', bright magenta-pink with darker veins and black-red centre, not such a strong grower as the other types. *G.* x *lindavicum* 'Alanah' (syn. *G. argenteum* 'Purpureum'), crimson-purple, free-flowering; 'Appleblossom', white, lightly veined with pale pink, silver grey foliage, raised by Blooms Nurseries in Norfolk. *G. argenteum*, pale pink to white with darker veins, silvery foliage.

Geranium cinereum **'Lawrence Flatman'**   BELOW: *Geranium subcaulescens*

GERANIUM PHAEUM AND RELATED TYPES

" I have said many times that if I did not have a woodland area in my garden with its attendant shade, then I would have to create one. And one very good reason is that I would need somewhere to grow Geranium phaeum *and its close relative* G. x monacense. *For me, these are geraniums of surpassing beauty, although in recommending them as warmly as I am able, I must add that there are gardeners who find them just too dark and sombre, and who have bought them on my recommendation and been disappointed. So to avoid an increase in my post, may I advise you to see the plants in flower before you buy; and then add simply that I hope you feel as I do. "*

Geranium phaeum

ORIGIN: Mountains of southern, central and eastern Europe such as the Pyrenees, Alps, Tatras and beyond. It has become naturalised in many northern areas, including Britain. where it is found in damp meadows, shady roadsides and at the edge of woodland. *G. phaeum* var. *lividum* is found in Croatia and extends as far west as the southern side of the French Alps.
SITE AND SOIL: All prefer partial or deep shade and can also, most usefully, tolerate fairly dry soils.
HARDINESS: Very hardy, tolerating -20°C (-4°F).
SIZE: 60 x 45cm (24 x 18in), the taller named forms can reach 75-90cm (30-36in).

SPECIAL FEATURES
Unusual dark-coloured flowers that appear from late spring to early summer, often with a smaller repeat performance in autumn. The plants are almost evergreen but, although often described as ground cover plants, they are really too tall for that role. However they are a stunning group of geraniums.

ABOVE: *Geranium phaeum*

BELOW: *Geranium phaeum* 'Album'

**Recommended varieties
and similar species:**

G. phaeum (dusky cranesbill or the mourning widow), purple-red or soft lilac, in both cases with a white base, several variants in different shades, soft green foliage, self-seeds, but not invasively; 'Album', large white flowers with golden anthers, named by Walter Ingwersen in 1946 from a plant collected in Switzerland, although I am amazed that this is the same species as it looks totally different to me; 'Joan Baker', very pale lavender with dark ring near the centre, a tall form found in Bill Baker's garden in Berkshire and named after his wife; 'Langthorn's Blue', blue, tall; 'Lily Lovell', large flowers of rich mauve, raised by Trevor Bath of Surrey and named after his mother; 'Mourning Widow' (syn. *G. phaeum* 'black'), crimson-black with golden anthers, tall; 'Rose Madder', brown-pink; 'Samobor', typical *G. phaeum* flowers but large leaves zoned with chocolate brown, a recent introduction by Washfield Nursery; 'Taff's Jester', typical *G. phaeum* flowers but the foliage has yellow-green and purple-brown markings; 'Variegatum', leaves marked with cream, red and pale green, shorter than most at 45cm (18in); var. *hungaricum*, maroon, tall; var. *lividum*, pale grey or lilac, flower colour varies; var. *lividum* 'Majus', a taller clone with larger flowers, discovered by Mrs Rogers of Bromley, Kent.

G. x monacense is a beautiful hybrid between *G. phaeum* and *G. reflexum*.

The cross seems to have occurred many times, although the plant was named after the City of Munich by Dr Kurt Harz who found it in his own Bavarian garden. The flowers are dull purple-pink with violet veins and a white central zone, but vary depending on the clone; 'Muldoon' (syn. *G. punctatum* Hort.), a stunning plant, undoubtedly among my three favourite geraniums, purple-brown blotches on the foliage; 'Variegatum' (syn. *G. punctatum* 'Variegatum'), similar to the original hybrid but with variegated foliage; var. *anglicum*, pink-lilac with blue-violet zone and strongly veined. *G. reflexum*, from Italy, Croatia and Greece is like *G. phaeum* but the flowers are smaller and slightly lighter coloured.

Geranium x *monacense* 'Muldoon'

Geranium aristatum

ORIGIN: Italy and southern Albania, former Yugoslavia and Greece.
SITE AND SOIL: Best in a sunny position but can tolerate partial shade.
HARDINESS: Very hardy, tolerating -20°C (-4°F).
SIZE: Forms a hummock 45-60cm (18-24in) tall.

SPECIAL FEATURES

The flowers are the palest lilac-pink to almost white with lilac veins. A distinctly hairy plant with grey-green foliage but unlike *G. phaeum*, not evergreen.

SOME ANNUAL AND BIENNIAL GERANIUMS

❝ *I think it is probably fair to say that the genera of most garden plants tend to be thought of either as annuals or as perennials. And I also know it is true that* Geranium *comes into the latter category, although in the old gardening books they were described not as perennials, but rather endearingly as 'abiding plants'. If, however, we think of our native species, one of the most familiar and common is actually an annual, herb Robert,* Geranium robertianum. *However, its ability to survive over winter does tend to give the impression that, like a perennial, it is always there. Even someone as enthusiastic about geraniums as I am is not going to try and convince you that they are important components of an annual bed, but I do think that in the wild garden, there are annual (and biennial) species that should certainly find a home.* ❞

Geranium lucidum

ORIGIN: Europe, North Africa, south west and central Asia. A British native found on shady rocks, walls and waste ground.
SITE AND SOIL: Will grow in most places including shade and dry soil, but best on alkaline soils.
HARDINESS: Hardy annual.
SIZE: Up to 40 x 30cm (16 x 12 in) from autumn sowings, plants sown in spring or on poor soil will be smaller.

SPECIAL FEATURES

Attractive glossy green rosettes which redden with age, stems also red. Small, deep pink flowers in spring and summer. Useful where little else will grow, in walls, sloping banks or in a wild garden. A prolific self-seeder.

RIGHT: *Geranium robertianum* 'Celtic White'
BELOW: *Geranium robertianum*

Geranium lucidum

Geranium rubescens

ORIGIN: Madeira, naturalised on Guernsey and the Isle of Man.
SITE AND SOIL: Sun or partial shade. Any reasonably fertile garden soil.
HARDINESS: Moderately hardy, tolerating -10°C (14°F).
SIZE: Up to 60cm (24in) tall.

SPECIAL FEATURES

Like a large form of *G. robertianum* with reddish stems, and leaves that turn red in autumn. Bright pink flowers with red eye and pale veins are produced from late spring to the autumn. Forms a good overwintering rosette. A biennial that is easy to raise from seed.

Geranium robertianum

ORIGIN: Thought to have come originally from eastern North America, but now widely distributed through Europe, the Himalayas and parts of Africa, Asia and China. A British plant often found in hedgerows; the reference to Robert seems to be an ancient one perhaps linked to *Knecht Ruprecht* the house goblin in Germany and Robin (diminutive of Robert) Goodfellow of England.
SITE AND SOIL: Sun or shade in any type of soil.
HARDINESS: Hardy annual that overwinters.
SIZE: Varies; some forms are compact.

SPECIAL FEATURES

Flowers continually, even in mild spells over winter. Succulent rosettes of ferny foliage on rather stiff, wiry stems, often reddish. Unpleasant smell, especially after rain and described as 'foxy'. Can be allowed to self-seed in walls, paving or wild area but too invasive for other parts of the garden.

Recommended Varieties

G. robertianum, small bright pink or white, ferny foliage, red tints to foliage and stems; 'Celtic White', tiny white flowers, a dwarf form with flat rosettes, light green ferny foliage, self-seeds.

Geranium bohemicum

ORIGIN: East and central Europe as far north as southern Scandinavia.
SITE AND SOIL: Thrives in most good garden soils; best in full sun or very light shade.
HARDINESS: Very hardy, tolerating -20°C (-4°F).
SIZE: 30 x 60cm (12 x 24in).

SPECIAL FEATURES

One of only a handful of annual and biennial geraniums to have blue flowers and for this reason, it's a mystery to me why it is so uncommon. A sprawling, hairy biennial, worth considering in a wild garden for its flower colour.

6 6 *One of the simplest distinctions between geraniums and pelargoniums is that the former are usually hardy in cool temperate climates while the latter are not. There are exceptions to most rules in horticulture however, and there are a few half-hardy geraniums. In addition, they happen to be such magnificent plants that I could not possibly leave them out of this book, even though only gardeners in mild and sheltered places will be able to sustain them outside all year round. They are big plants, and while they can be grown perfectly well under cover, it is important to have room to do so, and to be able to provide adequate warmth in winter for them to flourish properly.* 9 9

RIGHT: **Geranium palmatum**

BELOW: **Geranium canariense**

Geranium canariense

ORIGIN: Canary Isles. The similar, although not very closely related, G. palmatum originates from Madeira, but has been widely cultivated in Europe since the 18th century. It was introduced to Britain in 1778 but most books, certainly the older ones, refer to it as Geranium anemonifolium.

SITE AND SOIL: Needs a dry, sheltered corner in mild areas, and a well-drained soil. Alternatively, grow in a container and bring in to a green-house or conservatory to overwinter.

HARDINESS: Barely hardy, tolerating around 0°C to -5°C (32°F to 23°F). Will survive in a cold greenhouse overwinter.

SIZE: Usually 50-75 cm (20-30in) but mature plants growing outside can reach 90cm (36in) or more in favourable conditions.

SPECIAL FEATURES

A striking large rosette of glossy, fragrant 30cm (12in) wide leaves borne on a short stem. A short-lived perennial lasting around three years. It can be propagated by seed or sometimes it may produce new rosettes which will develop in situ, or may be removed for replanting elsewhere. Deep pink flowers in spring.

Geranium palmatum (syn. G. anemonifolium) (AGM), is similar to G. canariense but with a shorter stem and leaves up to 35cm (14in) wide. It is less commonly seen although I think probably a more attractive plant.

RIGHT: **Geranium maderense**

Geranium maderense

ORIGIN: Madeira, where it was seen in cultivation by Major C H C Pickering, who also located one of the few surviving wild populations, and introduced this species to Britain as recently as the 1950s. Its widespread cultivation now is due to his efforts.

SITE AND SOIL: Needs a cool greenhouse in most areas, where it is best grown in a soil border. When grown in a container it needs potting on frequently to avoid a check to growth. It can withstand summer drought and in very mild areas of Britain it will grow outdoors. I have seen it grown extensively outside in the Channel Islands, in the extreme south-west of the British mainland and also on the Scilly Isles, where conditions seem to suit it and it has become naturalised on the cliffs.

HARDINESS: Tender.

SIZE: Stem-bearing rosette is up to 60cm (24in) and 6cm (2in) in diameter. The leaves are up to 60cm (24 in)wide. It produces an inflorescence up to 1.2m (4ft) high.

The largest of all geraniums, and a quite magnificent plant when well grown. When suffering under marginal conditions, however, it becomes a sorry pest-ridden mess. It has a huge rosette of very large, sticky, aromatic leaves on pale brown stalks. The purple flowers are borne on tall inflorescences which, together with the centre of the rosette, become propped up by the old leaf stalks. It grows during autumn and winter and flowers from late winter to early spring onwards, little growth being made in summer. It flowers in its second or third year but is monocarpic and dies after flowering, though it may produce side shoots.

Pelargoniums

Pelargoniums are perennials, but because they are half-hardy, they are used in the garden in the same way as half-hardy annuals. In terms of their siting, this means that they are at home in beds and borders and also, and to my mind most significantly, in containers. That they are perennial raises the question of what should be done with them in the winter. I will come to that later (see page 52) but first, specifically, their use in the garden.

Using Pelargoniums in the Garden

I shall begin with containers because I believe that these offer the best way to grow and display all types of pelargonium. One sound reason is the purely pragmatic one of cost. No pelargonium is cheap, and while it might be practical for municipal corporations to plant up large beds with them, it is a outlay that most home gardeners would not be willing to entertain. Moreover, with the exception of the Dwarf and Miniature varieties, which are probably better used as houseplants, most pelargoniums are relatively large. A single plant of one of the Zonal varieties in a hanging basket, or two or three in a window box or tub will make a very effective display and provide a fine central feature around which other, lower-growing plants may be placed. Even with pendulous pelargoniums, (the Ivy-leaved varieties and 'Breakaway' types of Zonal), no more than three or four should be needed to create a considerable impact.

The scented-leaved and species pelargoniums have a considerable appeal but it is not derived from large and showy flowers. This is also true of many of the fancy-leaved Zonals where, although flowers may be present, they are of secondary appeal to the leaves. So once again, a small number of specimen plants in a container will draw special attention to them, and encourage people to inspect them more closely. Every summer, I use several large terracotta containers for my scented-leaved and species pelargoniums, packing up to ten plants, each still in their own individual pots, into each. And a very pleasing effect they produce when placed close to doors, seats or other places where people tend to linger. More information on planting, and using containers in the garden is in Book 8 of the series, *Best Container Plants*.

If you do use pelargoniums in large-scale plantings, either in big tubs containing many plants or even in open

ABOVE: *Pelargonium* 'Brocade'   **RIGHT:** *Pelargonium* 'Duke of Buckingham'

ground beds, be aware of the strength of their flower colours. Ask yourself why the traffic island opposite Buckingham Palace contains a mass of bright red Zonals every year. It is so that they can be appreciated by the Palace's residents from 100 meters or more away. Yes, most of the colours of the Zonal varieties and their smaller counterparts are pretty fierce. They will assert themselves from across your garden and *en masse*, can render almost everything else you grow pretty drab. In my own garden, I only use the red varieties in odd ones and twos for a particular effect. Larger containers, if they are filled with Zonals,

are filled only with pink and white varieties.

Most of the other familiar summer bedding plants blend perfectly well with pelargoniums, if you are careful with their colours. Silver foliaged helichrysum, white verbena, pink petunias, powder blue ageratum and rich blue lobelia all make fine companions with appropriately coloured pelargoniums. Where you will come seriously unstuck however, is if you begin mixing pelargoniums with the likes of orange African marigolds; even the so-called orange Zonals will not do here.

And finally, although it is rather

Pelargonium 'Deacon Suntan'

beyond the scope of this book, it is worth saying just how good pelargoniums are as house plants; indeed I think the Regals are so much better indoors than they are outside. But perhaps the way in which pelargoniums are least appreciated is as cut flowers. I discovered many years ago, when removing flowers from overwintering stock plants, that they keep in small vases for a long time without dropping or wilting. In winter especially, a few blooms on a table in a little cut-glass container can be both pretty and welcome.

Pelargonium **'Highfield Festival'**

Propagation

Pelargoniums are easy to propagate, either from cuttings or, in the case of the newer hybrid Zonal varieties, from seed. None are amenable to being divided. I will start with propagation by cuttings because this is still the commonest and most valuable method. Cuttings may be taken either in late summer or in early spring. In terms of rooting success, I do not find there is much difference between the times and the choice really depends on the facilities you have available and the expectations you have of the resultant plants. If you take cuttings at the end of the season, you will need somewhere to keep them, at a minimum temperature of around 7°C (45°F), through the winter. However, your plants should have formed good roots before the temperature begins to fall and thus will be quicker to flower in the spring than cuttings taken early in the year.

Cuttings may be taken from any strong shoots of the current season's growth. If you can not find a non-flowering shoot, simply snap the flowers off a flowering shoot. You should aim to obtain shoots about 10cm (4in) long. Cut them with a sharp knife just below a node (the swelling from which the leaves arise). Pull off the lowest pair of leaves and, if they are large, the next pair also. Dip the cut end of the shoots in a hormone rooting powder, knock off the excess powder and insert the cuttings to a depth of about 2 cm (¾in) in a tray of soil-based seedling/cutting compost. Cover with a propagator lid or similar ventilated cover and place in a light, warm place; a temperature of around 15°C (59°F) is ideal. Roots will form in about two weeks and after a further two weeks, the cuttings should be potted on into 7.5cm (3in) diameter individual pots.

Raising pelargoniums from seed is limited to the hybrid Zonal types (page 56). The seed is expensive but very reliable if adequate warmth is given; pelargoniums are among the plants that need high temperatures to germinate and if you do not provide this, your money will have been wasted. Most packets contain six or twelve seeds. The cost of an individual seed is therefore rather alarming, but it should be set against the value of the resultant plant; and of course the pleasure that you will have from raising it.

Seeds may be sown in late summer or late winter but careful calculations and trials by commercial growers (who know better than amateur gardeners about cost-effectiveness) have now shown that the former is to be preferred. If seeds are sown then, you will have strong plants by early winter. They can then be kept relatively cool until the spring and still flower in early summer. If the seeds are not sown until late winter, much higher temperatures (and hence higher costs) are required to produce good plants in time for the new season.

Sow the seeds about 5mm (¼in) deep in a soil-based seedling compost in a pot or seed tray. The optimum germination temperature is about 22°C (72°F) and at this the seed should germinate within seven days. Once germination has occurred, the temperature should be lowered to about 18°C (64°F) and after two more weeks, the plants should be pricked out into individual pots, just like the cuttings. They may then be grown in these pots at a minimum temperature of 7°C through the winter.

ABOVE: *Pelargonium* 'Magda'

RIGHT: *Pelargonium* 'King of Denmark'

Care

Pelargoniums are among the easiest of summer-flowering plants to care for, and that is part of their appeal. They are particularly valuable because they can survive relatively long periods without being watered, and are a boon to people who may be away from home for any length of time.

But the best results inevitably come from a plant that is given the best conditions in which to grow and I always use a soil-based potting compost for my pelargoniums during the summer. John Innes No 2 Potting Compost contains a valuable reserve of nutrients and does not dry out too quickly. This is also perfectly satisfactory for winter storage of both rooted cuttings or stock plants,

Pelargonium 'Polka'

although ideally I prefer to use John Innes No I which is less likely to encourage lush, soft growth.

Remember that pelargoniums have relatively soft tissues and, of course, that they are frost-tender. They should not be placed outside until after the danger of the last frost has passed and, just like all other plants being moved outside from the warmth of the greenhouse or home, must be hardened-off in a cold frame first. Similarly they must not be allowed to remain outside when the first frosts threaten. Nonetheless, an unexpected and early autumn frost is unlikely to be severe enough to kill them, though it may well scorch the tops. Pelargoniums are not in the same league of frost-tenderness as dahlias, nasturtiums or runner beans which blacken as soon as the temperature reaches 0°C.

The nutrients in a soil-based potting compost will be exhausted after six weeks during the summer and supplementary feeding, twice a week, should then begin with a proprietary liquid, or soluble, feed with a high potash content. Most general-purpose proprietary feeds satisfy this requirement, as does liquid tomato fertilizer. I have mentioned that pelargoniums are tolerant of dryness, but this does not mean they should be deliberately subjected to drought. As a rule water plants in hanging baskets daily, and plants in other containers every two days during the summer.

I have already touched on the fate of your plants in autumn and on page 51 explained that you may have rooted cuttings in the autumn and you will certainly have some mature plants. Even if there are cuttings available,

I always keep some big plants over winter to use as major features in the following year's plantings. After two years, though they become too big and woody to be used successfully for display, some may be kept longer as stock plants for cuttings. The scented-leaved and species pelargoniums especially can be kept for four or even five years although they too should then be replaced with new stock raised from cuttings.

Growing plants, whether cuttings or older, larger stock, should be overwintered in a greenhouse, conservatory or similar place. It is not necessary, nor desirable for them to grow much during the winter, and they should be kept relatively cool (about 7°C [45°F] is ideal). Do not attempt to store growing plants in a garage or similar, poorly lit place, the results will lead to disappointment.

At the end of summer, the top growth should be cut back. Gardeners vary in the severity with which they do this but I like to leave a plant about 15cm (6in) tall, and if necessary with the shoots and leaves thinned out to permit good air flow between. One of the chief enemies of pelargoniums in winter is *Botrytis* (grey mould), which is encouraged by a mass of foliage that remains damp once wet. During winter, the plants must not be fed, although feeding should begin as the days begin to lengthen in the spring. They must also be kept almost dry, and a little water given on perhaps no more than four or five occasions during the winter will be sufficient.

If you do not have anywhere well-lit that can be maintained at a minimum of 7°C (45°F), you must keep your plants

Pelargonium **'Patricia Andrea'**

in a dormant state and should store them dry. There are two main ways in which this can be done. I have achieved the best results by simply leaving the plants in their pots, in compost, and allowing them to dry off. The alternative is to remove the plants from the pots, pull off most of the foliage, brush off the compost from the roots, dust the plants with sulphur powder to protect them from fungal decay, and wrap them loosely, one plant at a time, in envelopes or packets made from several sheets of newspaper. Leave the top of the packets open and store them vertically in cardboard boxes in a cool, frost-free and dry place. You will be very fortunate if you do not lose some plants, but the bulk should survive until the spring when they should be cut back by half, potted up, given a little water and placed somewhere warm to begin growth again.

Pelargoniums have their fair share of pests and diseases but none are impossible to control. The biggest problems come with plants kept in greenhouses pending planting out, or plants kept in warmth – as houseplants for instance – all year round. It is then that whitefly can become a real nuisance, and because no chemical spray is completely effective, I still find the best approach is to examine individual houseplants regularly and pinch off affected leaves as soon as whitefly are seen. With a mass of plants in a greenhouse, adopt the same policy of scrutiny but combine this with the use of sticky yellow cards to trap the insects. If a large collection of plants is kept permanently in a greenhouse, the use of biological control may be worthwhile. Further information will be found in *Best Garden Doctor*. Aphids will attack pelargoniums, but I find they are seldom serious and may be checked by any of the modern aphid insecticides.

I have mentioned the importance of avoiding *Botrytis* on overwintering plants but if infection does occur, spray promptly with sulphur or an appropriate modern fungicide. Both indoors and out, the powdery, brown spots of rust disease may be found attacking pelargoniums. If spotted sufficiently early, it may be checked by removing affected leaves, but in the unlikely event of attacks becoming severe, use a proprietary fungicide recommended for rust.

Occasionally pelargonium plants may decline through virus contamination. Cuttings from these plants will also be contaminated and the stock should be disposed of and replaced with new, freshly bought plants. The most obvious symptoms of virus are curling, distortion and mottling on the leaves.

Pelargonium **'Queen of Denmark'**

ZONAL PELARGONIUMS

" *The Zonal pelargonium is the classic, archetypal 'potted geranium'. It is the plant that adorns windowsills in children's paintings and picture books as much as it adorns gardens, houses, courtyards and patios in real life. Where would we be without them? To which the answer must be, wherever we were before the beginning of the eighteenth century. Because the Zonal pelargonium of today (usually called* P. x hortorum), *in all its manifestations, is largely the result of crosses between two South African species, the pink or white flowered* Pelargonium zonale *and the scarlet flowered* Pelargonium inquinans, *although some other, related species, have also been involved. Both* Pelargonium zonale *and* Pelargonium inquinans *were introduced to Britain in about 1710 although it seems that* Pelargonium zonale *had been in Holland for a considerable time before that. The presence of the two species in cultivation together however, inevitably prompted exper- imentation and hybridisation that has continued unabated to the present.*

Zonal pelargoniums form the largest group of pelargoniums in cultivation and they are usually further subdivided according to their foliage and flowers. The name 'zonal' comes from the dark horseshoe-shaped zone found on the leaves (and derived from Pelargonium zonale) *although some, such as white-flowered varieties and most of the modern F1 hybrids grown from seed, do not have this patterning, and so the name can be rather misleading. Within the overall Zonal group, those varieties that have golden foliage, crinkled leaves, white margins or white and red markings are now grouped together as 'fancy-leaved'. The rest are divided into those with single or double (or in reality, often semi-double) flowers. Seed-raised F1 hybrids are commonest in garden centres and seed catalogues, and may be obtained either as seed for raising yourself (page 51) or, with increasing popularity, as young plantlets. For the older varieties that can only be propagated by cuttings, you will need to buy from one of the excellent specialist suppliers.* "

Pelargonium 'Distinction'

ORIGIN: Exact parentage not known but it is thought that *P. zonale*, *P. inquinans* and *P. hybridum* were used to produce the first hybrids. Among older varieties still popular, 'Paul Crampel' was bred by the French nurseryman Pierre Lemoine in 1889, but many of the varieties were raised more recently. Ken Gamble in England bred many in the 1970s and 1980s, including the popular 'Highfield' range.
SIZE: Varies from 30cm (12in) up to 90cm (36in).

AVAILABLE COLOUR RANGE
Orange, pinks, reds, purples and white.

SPECIAL FEATURES
Single-flowered varieties have five petals, usually of equal size. Indispensable outdoors as summer bedding, either in the ground or in containers. The flowers are more resistant to weather damage than the double varieties.

Recommended Varieties
'Ashfield Serenade' (AGM), lavender-pink, compact; 'Caledonia', pale mauve; 'Christopher Ley', bright orange-red; 'Crampel's Master', compact version of 'Paul Crampel' (below); 'Distinction', red, very dark, almost black edge to the foliage; 'Dryden', pale scarlet and white bicolour; 'Edward Humphris', white; 'Elizabeth Angus', rose with white eye, vigorous; 'Francis James', magenta-pink with white edge veined with pink; 'Highfield's Choice', lavender-pink, ball-shaped blooms; 'Highfield's Symphony', pink shading to salmon; 'Mr Wren', orange-red petals edged with white; 'New Life', red and white variegated stripes, sometimes throws out pale pink flowers; 'Paul Crampel', scarlet, old variety; 'Prince of Wales', magenta with scarlet eye; 'Skelly's Pride', soft salmon, fringed petals, tall; 'The Boar', salmon-pink, a straggly habit ideal for hanging baskets or urns.

ABOVE: *Pelargonium* 'Mr Wren'

RIGHT: *Pelargonium* 'Paul Crampel'

ZONAL SINGLES (FROM SEED)

" Popular as the traditional zonal pelargonium was, it had drawbacks, especially for commercial horticulture. The fact that plants had to be raised vegetatively, by cuttings, was highly labour-intensive if it was to satisfy the demand from municipal Parks departments for their vast bedding schemes. And many stocks of traditional varieties degenerated through virus contamination. Although numerous other bedding plants were, and are, available, the public still wanted its pelargoniums. The situation was rescued with the development at Pennsylvania State University, in 1965, of the first pelargonium hybrids that could be raised from seed to produce predictable plants. This enabled tens of thousands of plants to be produced with significantly less labour, although, at least initially, not at a great saving in cost. The high temperatures needed to induce seed germination in winter, and then grow on the young plants to ensure flowering early in the summer, can be a costly process. The tendency now among commercial growers however, is to sow in autumn and maintain the plants at fairly high temperature until they are pricked on. They are then grown on over winter in cooler conditions when they will produce flowers by late spring (page 51). "

Pelargonium 'Multibloom Mixed'

ORIGIN: Bred by seed companies in Britain and elsewhere. Varieties that have similar flowering times and growth habits are grouped together into Series and each member of the Series should have a distinct flower colour. The seeds may be sold as a collection of mixed colours or single colours may be offered.
SIZE: 30-35cm (12-14in).

AVAILABLE COLOUR RANGE

Formerly limited to vivid red and white, but an increasingly wide range has now become available. Within each series there is usually a red, pink, salmon and a lighter colour such as 'apple-blossom'. Most series contain a white, but these are often inferior in habit to the other colours. Few individual varieties remain available for many years, as new and better forms are constantly being produced. The range is still relatively limited and for many gardeners, including myself, these plants are bland compared with the true old zonals. But they have a valuable role to play and clearly, they are here to stay.

SPECIAL FEATURES

The more recent seed-raised pelargoniums have a greater colour range and produce more flowers than the first of the modern seed-raised varieties like 'Sprinter'. As an alternative to raising them yourself, many of these varieties may now be bought as seedlings or small plants from garden centres or by mail order.

Most seed-raised pelargoniums are F1 hybrids which produce uniform, vigorous plants with numerous flowers,

Pelargonium **'Century Deep Salmon'**

they are ideal subjects for containers or beds close to the house. F1 hybrids are expensive to produce however, so for bedding out large areas, the F2 hybrids are worth considering. These offer less uniformity than the F1 hybrids but the seeds cost about half the price.

Pelargonium **'Breakaway Salmon'**

Recommended Varieties

Standard or specimen types
These have single flowers in a few fairly large heads for optimum impact. They can be planted in small to medium sized beds or in containers. 'Century' Series (AGM), presently thirteen colours, the largest colour range; 'Hollywood Star' (AGM), deep rose-pink and white bicolour, the rest of the 'Hollywood' series is no longer available; 'Horizon Deep Scarlet', a good single colour from a series that has reasonably weather resistant flowers; 'Maverick Star' blush pink with deeper edges and a rose eye, many new colours are now available in this series but none are bicolours,

uniform flowering on short stems and ideal for containers; 'Orange Appeal', the first truly orange hybrid to be raised from seed, large flower heads of rich orange; 'Orbit' Series, eight colours including shades such as 'apple-blossom', not as uniform in habit as some of the other series but flowers well.

Cascading types These are half-way between standard and trailing types with branches bearing individual flowers arching outwards from the base. Use them as single subjects in hanging baskets or in tall containers. In large numbers, they can look stunning. One series dominates: 'Breakaway' Series, available in red or

salmon, a flat spreading habit that branches readily from the base.

Multibloom (Floribunda) types
Masses of flowering stems, up to ten on each plant at any time are produced, and each flower head is open in habit so there are less problems with *Botrytis* because air can circulate between the petals. 'Multibloom', eight colours, early to flower but the series is not very uniform in height; 'Sensation' Series, five colours, early to flower.

Dwarf bedding types 'Vista' Series, four single colours, an F2 worth considering for bedding out large areas.

ZONAL DOUBLES (PLAIN-LEAVED)

" *Because of the advent, in recent years, of seed-raised hybrid pelargoniums, many gardeners do not seem to appreciate that the breeding of vegetatively propagated double-flowered varieties also continues apace. Although few breeders now go back to the original parent species (see right) for their source material, it is possible to develop new varieties by crossing existing ones. And of course, there is still a handful of older varieties that have retained their popularity, and failed to deteriorate with virus. Although fully double-flowered plants will normally produce no pollen, and cannot therefore be used as parents, it is generally possible to induce at least a few single flowers to form, complete with stamens and pollen. This can most simply be done by subjecting the plants to some form of stress, commonly by growing them in rather impoverished conditions. I should also mention one additional method by which a number of very good new, double flowered pelargonium varieties have been developed. This is simply by nurserymen spotting the occasional natural mutations that arise and then taking cuttings and perpetuating the abnormality. And it is appropriate here to pay special tribute to the many amateur breeders who have contributed so valuably to the range of excellent pelargoniums that we have today. The Deacon series (page 60) is among the best examples of these.* "*

ORIGIN: Exact parentage not known but it is thought that *P. zonale*, *P. inquinans* and *P. hybridum* were used to produce the first hybrids. Since then many varieties have been raised both by amateur and commercial breeders and some of the main groups are described below.
SIZE: 30-90cm (12-36in).

AVAILABLE COLOUR RANGE

Orange, pinks, purples, reds and white.

SPECIAL FEATURES

The large, showy flowers are the main attraction. Doubles have eight or more petals while semi-doubles have between five and eight. Both can only be grown from cuttings, not from seed. Use for bedding out, or as specimens in the centre of a hanging basket or container. The 'Irene' types have a strong bushy growth that overwinters well from autumn cuttings producing early-flowering plants.

Pelargonium 'Brocade'

Pelargonium 'Lady Ilchester'

Recommended Varieties

'Alpine Glow', white with pale magenta edge to each petal; 'Ashfield Monarch' (AGM), semi-double, bright red, compact habit; 'Beatrix', fuchsia purple; 'Bravo', soft orange with white centre; 'Brenda Kitson', bright rose-pink; 'Brocade', soft red shading to white in the centre; 'Burgenlandmädel' (often listed as 'Burgenland Girl' in nursery catalogues), coral-salmon; 'Crimson Fire', semi-double, scarlet; 'Diana Palmer', pink-red with serrated edges to petals; 'Dodd's Super Double', mid-red, almost a rosebud type (page 62); 'Downlands', salmon-pink; 'Duke of Buckingham', orange-scarlet; 'Emperor Nicholas', white edged with rose-red; 'Garnet', dark red; 'Gräfin Mariza' (syn. 'Countess Mariza'), coral to salmon-pink; 'Gustav Emich', red, the variety once planted outside Buckingham Palace because it matched the guardsmen's tunics, an old variety from 1898 but now supplanted in London by newer seed-raised varieties; 'Hermione', white; 'Hildegard', semi-double, orange-red; 'King of Denmark', pale salmon-pink, an old variety from 1877; 'Lady Ilchester', silver-pink; 'Magda', pale pink with scarlet markings; 'Mrs Lawrence', double, soft pink with satin-like appearance; 'Orange Ricard', semi-double, orange; 'Paul Humphries', deep crimson; 'Queen of Denmark', semi-double, deep salmon-pink; 'Regina', apple-blossom pink with salmon shading; 'Santa Maria', semi-double, salmon-pink; 'Shimmer', soft apricot with white centre; 'Sister Teresa', pure white; 'Snowmass', white; 'Something Special', pale salmon-pink; 'Summer Cloud', semi-double, white; 'Patricia Andrea', salmon-pink, an American variety with unusual, tulip-shaped flowers, sometimes listed in a separate 'Tulip-flowered' group.

Pelargonium **'Duke of Buckingham'**

Deacon Series These were bred by the late Rev. Stanley Stringer in Suffolk, England in the 1960s and 1970s and released from 1970 onwards. They are often listed as dwarf or semi-dwarf varieties but their size can vary greatly depending on the pot size used. In 10cm (4in) pots they can be kept at 20cm (8in) high but they can reach 90cm (36in) in a 45cm (18in) pot. They are sturdy plants with double flowers in a good range of colours from pastel to rich, intense shades. A mass of rather small flowers is produced over a long period. Of the 30 or so named varieties available from specialists today, you are most likely to come across the following:

'Deacon Arlon', white, often listed under dwarf varieties, not a strong grower, better grown in greenhouse; 'Deacon Birthday', salmon overlaid with peach; 'Deacon Bonanza', bright rose-pink; 'Deacon Constancy', light pastel pink; 'Deacon Coral Reef', coral pink; 'Deacon Fireball', scarlet; 'Deacon Lilac Mist', pale lilac-pink; 'Deacon Picotee', white with pale magenta edging; 'Deacon Regalia', ruby-red; 'Deacon Romance', bright pink; 'Deacon Sunburst', bright orange; 'Deacon Suntan', apricot-orange; 'Deacon Trousseau', salmon-pink.

Those with coloured foliage such as 'Deacon Minuet' are described on page 66.

Highfield pelargoniums The 'Highfield' range was raised in England by Ken Gamble in the 1970s and 1980s and includes single, double and semi-double flowers. The plants are sturdy with a compact habit and large flower heads.

Pelargonium **'Highfield Festival'**

'Highfield's Always', cream-white shading to pink in the centre; 'Highfield's Appleblossom', apple-blossom pink; 'Highfield's Attracta', white with pink edges and salmon centre; 'Highfield's Contessa', deep pink; 'Highfield's Fancy', purple-rose; 'Highfield's Festival', pale rose-pink; 'Highfield's Joy', pink, golden foliage with a good zone; 'Highfield's Prima Donna', deep rose-pink; 'Highfield's Sugar Candy', cream-white to pale pink.

Irene pelargoniums Irene zonals were first grown by Charles Behringer in Ohio in the USA in 1942. He named one of the early plants after his wife Irene and then used this as the parent for many other varieties. All have semi-double flowers.

'Corsair' (AGM), light red; 'Dark Red Irene', dark red; 'Electra', bright rose-pink; 'Genie', coral-pink; 'Penny', mid-pink; 'Rose Irene', rose-pink with white eye; 'Springtime', mid-pink; 'Trulls Hatch', salmon-pink.

Pelargonium **'King of Denmark'**

Pelargonium **'Deacon Suntan'**

ZONAL DOUBLES (PLAIN-LEAVED)

PAC

If you find this prefix to a variety name, it means that it was raised by a German commercial breeder Wilhelm Elsner of Dresden. These varieties come from a breeding programme in which the aim is to develop uniform, compact plants with good flowering impact and weather resistance. Their flowers are either semi-double or double. Many new varieties are released each year but look out especially for: 'Fox', crimson-purple and 'Ivalo', rose-pink.

Rosebud types In common with many other gardeners, I find these particularly appealing. They have tight clusters of double blooms, and are sometimes called Noisette pelargoniums. Their origin is unknown but there are references to them in literature that dates from one hundred years ago. They really need to be grown under cover to protect the flowers which collect water among their petals. 'Appleblossom Rosebud', white with pink edge to the petals and a green centre, one of the older varieties, dating back to 1870; 'Black Pearl', dark red, almost black; 'Pink Rambler', pale pink; 'Pink Rosebud'; 'Plum Rambler', purple; 'Purple Rambler'; 'Red Rambler', brick red; 'Scarlet Rambler'. Two striking new varieties of Rosebud pelargonium have patterned leaves: 'Westdale Appleblossom', white with pink edges to the petals, silver leaf variegation; and 'Happy Appleblossom', white with pink edges to the petals, lime green leaf patterning.

Pelargonium **'Magda'**

Pelargonium **'Queen of Denmark'**

Pelargonium 'Patricia Andrea'

ZONAL DOUBLES (FANCY-LEAVED)

" I am not alone among gardeners in believing that this group includes some of the greatest glories of the entire genus Pelargonium. Strangely however, they are still curiosities for many members of the public who have seen, at most, three or four varieties. Indeed, many people first see them in their school biology classes, and then seldom again, because the variegated Pelargonium leaf is a favourite with biology teachers. They use it to demonstrate the way that photosynthesis and starch production take place in the green but not the white parts of the leaf. It is always worth remembering that, in general, the greater the variegation (or at least, the greater the white part which lacks chlorophyll), the weaker will be the leaf, and the plant as a whole. Quite commonly these fancy-leaved Zonals mutate to produce leaves that are almost entirely white.

At its simplest, the group can be subdivided into bicolours which have leaves of green and white, and tricolours which have a more complex range of at least three colours including greens, reds, gold and cream, with a darker zone overlying them. The colours of the tricolours can be stunningly beautiful and extremely varied. The range of colours is produced very simply however: greater or lesser amounts of green chlorophyll, red anthocyanin and orange carotene are the principal pigments responsible. The colours tend to be strongest and most effective if the plants are spared full sun and although I do use them in the open garden, I always try to place them in containers that are in at least dappled shade. In my shaded greenhouse they achieve the most spectacular results. "

ORIGIN: Cultivated for nearly 250 years, the first are thought to have been natural sports of *P. inquinans*. Between 1853 and 1868, Peter Grieve of Bury St Edmunds in England raised a number of hybrids such as 'Lass O'Gowrie' and 'Mr Henry Cox' which are still worth growing. Modern raisers include Alan Shellard who has bred some good tricolours like 'Bette Shellard' (1991) and 'Falkland's Hero' (1983). Breeders are constantly trying to produce double-flowered tricolours, like 'Lucy Gunnett' (1989) which was bred by the late Bill Gunnett and named after his wife.
SIZE: 15–45cm (6–18in).

AVAILABLE COLOUR RANGE
Foliage colour ranges from bicolours (green and white) to tricolours (green, white and red) and gold with or without a bronze zone. Flower colour is usually red or salmon-pink.

SPECIAL FEATURES
The foliage on these plants is the main decorative feature. They do flower but these tend to be smaller than other zonals and, in the case of the tricolours, usually single. If you want impact from both flowers and foliage, my advice is to look first at the bicolours, as these often have plenty of single or double flowers. Use them as bedding or as indoor pot plants. They grow fairly slowly and as the best colours are on the youngest leaves it is worth pinching the shoots out regularly to encourage more new growth.

Pelargonium 'Ben Franklin'

Pelargonium 'Dolly Varden'

Pelargonium 'Frank Headley'

ZONAL DOUBLES (FANCY-LEAVED)

Recommended Varieties

'Ben Franklin' (AGM), double, soft mid-pink, bicolour; 'Bildeston', very pale pink with deep salmon eye, green and gold foliage; 'Blazonry', red, tricolour; 'Bristol', red, tricolour; 'Bronze Corinne', double, deep salmon-pink, golden to bronze foliage; 'Caroline Schmidt' (AGM), double, red, bicolour, first grown in 1880; 'Chelsea Gem', double, pale pink, crinkled leaves, bicolour; 'Cherie Maid', white with coral-pink veins, bicolour; 'Cherry Sundae', double, bright cherry-red, bicolour; 'Contrast', red, tricolour; 'Crystal Palace Gem', coral-rose, yellow-green with green markings; 'Deacon Peacock', double, orange-red, green and yellow foliage; 'Dolly Varden (AGM), scarlet, tricolour; 'Falkland's Hero', clear red, tricolour; 'Flower of Spring' (AGM), scarlet, bicolour; 'Frank Headley' (AGM), salmon-pink, bicolour; 'Freak of Nature', red, unusual bicolour as the main foliage colour is cream-white with green edges, slow-growing, usually grown as indoor pot plant; 'Friary Wood', double, purple, golden bronze foliage; 'Golden Brilliantissimum', double, cherry-red, tricolour; 'Golden Crest', rose-pink, rather sparse flowers, golden yellow foliage, slow-growing, semi-dwarf; 'Golden Harry Hieover', red, bronze-green foliage, spreading habit so ideal for urns; 'Happy Thought' (syn. 'A Happy Thought'), bright red, green with yellow centre; 'Hills of Snow', pale mauve, bicolour; 'Hurdy-Gurdy', double, crimson, tricolour; 'Ivory Snow', double,

Pelargonium 'Golden Harry Hieover'

Pelargonium 'Miss Burdett Coutts'

cream-white, bicolour; 'Lass O'Gowrie', pale rose-pink, tricolour; 'Lucy Gunnett', double, cerise, tricolour; 'Marechal MacMahon', red, deep bronze foliage; 'Merry-Go-Round', cherry-red, tricolour, slow-growing; 'Miss Burdett Coutts', red, tricolour; 'Mont Blanc', white, grey-silver foliage; 'Mr Henry Cox' (AGM), often misleadingly listed as 'Mrs H. Cox', pale pink, a bright and classic old tricolour which many gardeners find unbeatable; 'Mrs J C Mappin' (AGM), white, foliage silver with cream band; 'Mrs Parker', rose-pink, silver foliage; 'Mrs Pollock', orange, tricolour; 'Mrs Quilter', pink, gold and bronze foliage; 'Mrs Strang', orange-red, tricolour; 'Pink Golden Harry Hieover', the same as 'Golden Harry Hieover' but with pink flowers; 'Pink Happy Thought', the same as 'Happy Thought' but with pink flowers; 'Platinum', dawn-pink, bicolour; 'Preston Park', salmon-pink, green scalloped leaves edged with black zone; 'Princess Alexandra', double, mauve-pink, unusual bicolour with grey-green foliage and narrow silver-white edging; 'Sante Fe', salmon-pink, golden bronze foliage; 'Silver Wings', lavender, bicolour, compact; 'Skies of Italy', salmon-pink, tricolour, maple-shaped leaves; 'Sophie Dumaresque', red, tricolour; 'Stadt Bern', scarlet, very dark foliage (often listed as a dwarf variety in catalogues); 'Susie Q', soft pink, large flowers, golden bronze.

Pelargonium 'Happy Thought'

STELLAR-FLOWERED PELARGONIUMS

Stellar flowered, literally 'star-like' pelargoniums, are a fairly old group that originated in Australia, though they have become more popular in Britain recently with the introduction of newer, better varieties. They have distinctive pointed petals giving a dainty, if spiky, appearance. However I think that the 'stellar' of the name really refers to the leaves and not the flowers. I have never been certain of their ancestry and it seems to be something of a closely guarded secret although I cannot believe that they do not share at least something of their origin with the cactus varieties which I have placed with them. For convenience I have included here the recent 'Startel' range of F1 hybrids which are also Australian and rather similar, at least to the older stellar types.

ORIGIN: The early varieties were bred in Australia by the late Ted Both. Since then, other breeders such as Ian Gillam have introduced improved forms in the 1980s.
SIZE: Varies, some varieties could be classed as dwarfs or miniatures; 13cm (5in) to 45cm (18in).

AVAILABLE COLOUR RANGE

Bicolours, orange, pinks, reds and white. Varieties also available with golden foliage.

SPECIAL FEATURES

Maple-shaped leaves with dark zones make an attractive foil to the flowers. The flowers have narrow petals, giving them a dainty, sometimes almost spidery appearance. They can be grown outside and as indoor pot plants. If they are to be grown outdoors, however, they should really be in containers in a sheltered spot as the flowers are easily spoiled by rain.

Recommended Varieties
'Arctic Star', white; 'Bird Dancer' (AGM), pale pink, dwarf, a striking and always popular plant; 'Dawn Star', pale pink; 'Fire Dragon', scarlet; 'Gemini', scarlet and white; 'Golden Ears', vermilion, stellar type, pale green foliage with brown blotch, compact, one of my special favourites; 'Golden Staphs', salmon-orange, golden foliage; 'Grenadier' (syns. 'Lady Alice of Valencia', 'Stellar Grenadier'), (AGM), double, crimson, unzoned green foliage; 'Hannaford Star' (syn. 'Stellar Hannaford Star'), deep salmon-pink; 'Pagoda', double, pink-white; 'Supernova', double, lilac-pink shading to white; 'Vancouver Centennial' (AGM), brick-red, bronze and gold foliage (a very popular variety that is listed as dwarf or fancy-leaved in some catalogues). 'Startel' F1 hybrids have large ball-shaped heads comprising many flowers with four or five-pointed petals in a range of reds and pinks. They should be raised from seed in the same way as other F1 hybrids (page 51).

LEFT: *Pelargonium* 'Pagoda'

RIGHT: *Pelargonium* 'Spitfire'

CACTUS-FLOWERED PELARGONIUMS

So-called cactus-flowered varieties exist in several different groups of garden plants, the best known are dahlias. I am not sure how the designation arose because while the flowers are spiky, they do not look a great deal like the flowers of real cacti -perhaps it is their spines that they are supposed to emulate. They are sometimes called poinsettia-flowered but I find this no more logical. Whatever the origin of the name, which seems to be a fairly recent invention, the origin of the cactus-flowered varieties of pelargonium themselves is also obscure. Varieties of this type were illustrated and listed in catalogues at the beginning of the 20th century and I have always imagined they are British or at least European in origin.

Pelargonium 'Fascination'

ORIGIN: The exact origin is unknown but varieties of this type were listed in catalogues at the turn of the century.
SIZE: Varies, up to 45cm (18in).

AVAILABLE COLOUR RANGE

Orange, pinks, reds, purple and white.

SPECIAL FEATURES

The flowers are undeniably unusual. The petals are furled inwards like quills. They are best grown indoors as pot plants, or where they can be given overhead protection because they are prone to rain damage.

Recommended Varieties
'Cherry', double, cherry-red; 'Fascination', carmine; 'Mini-Czech', ruby-red, deep green zoned foliage, dwarf; 'Mrs Salter Bevis, double, light pink; 'Noel', double, white; 'Spitfire', double, orange-red, foliage is green edged with cream; 'Star of Persia', double, magenta.

ANGEL PELARGONIUMS

I find the angels quite compelling. I cannot imagine why they are called angels unless it is from the name of the first, which happened to be 'Angeline'. But, by the reasoning that gave us cactus or poinsettia-flowered varieties, pansy or viola-flowered would seem far more relevant. Viola would be appropriate, not only for the appearance of the flowers but because most of the varieties that I have seen are violet or purple in colour. I find they always look best in containers with others of their type and they do not blend well with other types of plant, nor even with other forms of pelargonium. But a single pot of angels will turn heads.

ORIGIN: The first angel pelargonium, 'Angeline', was listed in the 1820s but it was not until the 1930s that new varieties began to be introduced by Langley Smith of Catford, London. They are sometimes listed as miniature regals and although they do have a superficial resemblance to the regals, they have a different ancestry. 'Angeline' was used with *P. crispum* and *P. grossularioides* to produce plants with neat, crinkled foliage. Modern breeders have extended the colour range; for example, Jan Taylor produced 'Tip Top Duet', Velvet Duet' and 'Wayward Angel' all three with AGMs, and Harry Selley named varieties after Devon rivers like 'The Tone' and 'The Mole'.
SIZE: 25cm (10in).

AVAILABLE COLOUR RANGE

Mostly pinks and purple; no reds.

SPECIAL FEATURES

The flowers look like pansies and as a mass of blooms are produced, these can be very eye-catching plants, though the leaves are small. The plants benefit from frequent pinching out to create a bushy habit and, used indoors, several can effectively be planted in a bowl or pot.

Pelargonium **'Mrs G. H. Smith'**

ABOVE: *Pelargonium* **'Swilland'**   RIGHT: *Pelargonium* **'Catford Bell'**

Recommended Varieties

'Captain Starlight', upper petals purple-crimson, lower petals mauve; 'Catford Belle' (AGM), mauve-pink with deep maroon blotch, one of the oldest angels; 'Darmsden' (AGM), deep maroon upper petals, dusky rose-pink lower petals; 'Fairy Orchid', white with pink blush on edge of upper petals, frilled blooms; 'Kettle Baston' (AGM), upper petals royal purple, lower petals mauve-pink, the curious name is that of a Suffolk village; 'Lara Maid'* (AGM), white with purple blotches, tall; 'Madame Layal'*, purple and white, small flowers; 'Mairi', white and pale purple; 'Manx Maid'*, plum-purple on pink base, tall; 'Moon Maiden', light rose marked with deeper rose; 'Mrs G H Smith', white with pink markings, compact; 'Needham Market', pale mauve with deep purple markings; 'Raspberry Ripple', pink with the upper petals a deeper pink; 'Rietje van der Lee', white with pink-mauve markings; 'Rita Scheen', white with purple markings, variegated foliage; 'Rose Bengal', upper petals purple, lower petals mauve-pink; 'Seeley's Pansy'*, white with royal purple blotch on upper petals, small flowers; 'Spanish Angel' (AGM), upper petal almost black with picotee edge, lower petals are lilac with dark purple markings; 'Spring Park', lilac with purple blotch on upper petals, flowers early; 'Swedish Angel', deep purple with white edges and markings, rather large flowers, slow-growing; 'Swilland', royal velvet upper petals, lower petals are pink with purple blotch, small flowers; 'Tip Top Duet' (syn. 'Lord de Ramsey') (AGM), upper petals magenta, lower petals mauve, a striking plant that people always comment on in my garden; 'Variegated Madame Layal'* (AGM), purple and white flowers with silver variegated foliage; 'Velvet Duet' (AGM), deep purple, lax stems so best grown in a basket; 'Wayward Angel' (AGM), mauve flowers with purple blotch on upper petals.

* Some experts prefer not to classify these varieties as angels as they have a different origin. Strictly they are old-style regals but are also different from modern regals (page 86). They are often called 'Decorative Pelargoniums'.

UNIQUE PELARGONIUMS

" *It could be said that each group of pelargoniums is uniquely different from all other groups so why these should have been singled out is not obvious. They are among the older groups and are commonly mentioned and illustrated in nineteenth century gardening books. They are big plants with small flowers and, to be honest, I do not find they are at their best in most British gardens. The problem is simply their size. A small unique is a pathetic thing, but a big unique is generally too big to keep over winter in a normal sized greenhouse. They may be cut back hard at the end of the season and will certainly put on plenty of fresh growth in the next, but you cannot reduce the size of the container. Nonetheless, if they are given space, both in summer and winter, they can be very impressive.* "

ORIGIN: Uniques are mentioned in nursery catalogues dating back to the early nineteenth century and they were certainly popular with Victorian gardeners. They are thought to have been developed from *P. fulgidum*.

SIZE: Varies up to 45cm (18in).

AVAILABLE COLOUR RANGE

Pinks, reds, purple and white.

SPECIAL FEATURES

Large plants with woody stems. The flowers are bright and rather like small regals. The foliage is scented but can be pleasant or unpleasant. They can be used as bedding or to fill gaps in herbaceous or mixed borders but they will not tolerate heavy rain. They look very effective tumbling out of urns, hanging baskets or window boxes, provided they are in a sheltered position.

Pelargonium '**Clorinda**'

Pelargonium '**Crimson Unique**'

Recommended Varieties

'Bolero', mid-pink with red blotch, a cross between a unique and a regal; 'Carefree', red-pink overlaid with scarlet; 'Claret Rock Unique', claret-red, dark foliage, strong grower; 'Clorinda', rose-pink, cedar-scented foliage (often listed with scented-leaved varieties); 'Crimson Unique' (AGM), deep crimson with black markings, large flowers; 'Golden Clorinda', bright pink, gold and green foliage (often listed with scented-leaved varieties); 'Hula', mid-pink with a deeper blotch, another cross between a unique and a regal; 'Jessel's Unique', neon-rose with purple veins; 'Monsieur Ninon', crimson, frilled flowers, well-divided foliage; 'Mrs Kingsbury', light magenta; 'Paton's Unique' (AGM), crimson-pink with maroon veins; 'Polka', orange-red with purple markings; 'Purple Unique', purple-mauve, large flowers, aromatic foliage; 'Rollisson's Unique', bright magenta-red; 'Scarlet Pet', red with black veins; 'Scarlet Unique', bright scarlet, fast-growing with pungent scent; 'Shrubland Pet', deep pink with dark blotches; 'Unique Aurore' (syns. 'Aurore Unique', 'Aurore'), white with coppery crimson markings, grey-green foliage, upright habit; 'Voodoo', light burgundy with purple-black throat, compact; 'White Unique' white, free-flowering, dense foliage.

Pelargonium **'Polka'**

DWARF PELARGONIUMS

" *Most groups of garden flowers have small varieties and pelargoniums are no exception. I confess to being slightly cautious about including them as separate, however, even though most nursery catalogues do so. For me, they just are not a distinct enough group. While most are small versions of the normal single and double Zonals, there are also small ivy-leaved and other types and, at the end of the day, all one can really say is that they are small. I suppose they are a useful assemblage for people with small gardens; or indeed small homes because they do make excellent window-sill plants, incidentally making good companions for the small types of African violet.* "

ABOVE: *Pelargonium 'Sugar Baby'*   BELOW: *Pelargonium 'Mr Everaarts'*

ORIGIN: Most varieties listed today are modern, having originated in the 1980s and 1990s with a few from the 1960s. One of the oldest is 'Friesdorf' raised by Lobner in 1927.
SIZE: 20-30cm (8-12in), varieties over 25cm (10in) are sometimes described as semi-dwarf.

AVAILABLE COLOUR RANGE

Pinks, reds and white.

SPECIAL FEATURES

The neat, branching habit makes them ideal for small areas, both indoors or outside. They are particularly useful for window boxes and, being compact, they can withstand winds.

Pelargonium 'Turkish Delight'

Recommended Varieties

'Alcyone', medium-pink, large flowers; 'Cameo', semi-double, rich carmine-rose with white throat; 'Coddenham', double, bright orange-red, long stems, zoned foliage; 'Dame Anna Neagle' (AGM), double, pale powder pink; 'Dolly Read', white with pink centre and white eye, dark green foliage; 'Dovedale', semi-double, white, golden foliage; 'Elizabeth Read', lavender-pink with white eye; 'Emma Jane Read', double, deep mauve-pink, dark green foliage; 'Fantasie' (AGM), double, white, free-flowering; 'Fleurette', double, coral-to salmon-pink, deep green zoned foliage, one of the oldest dwarf varieties; 'Friesdorf', red overlaid with crimson, dark green foliage with black zone, semi-dwarf, growth can be spindly; 'Gay Baby', pale mauve, small flowers, the first miniature ivy-leaved variety; 'High Tor', double, apple-blossom pink, copper zone on foliage, semi-dwarf; 'Hope Valley' (AGM), double, rose-pink, yellow-green foliage with pale zone; 'Little Alice' (AGM), double, bright salmon-pink, dark green foliage; 'Marmalade', double, orange-red, long stems, a Californian variety; 'Monica Bennett', fuchsia-pink with darker veins, dark foliage with darker zone; 'Morval' (AGM), double, soft blush pink, golden yellow foliage with darker zone; 'Mr Everaarts', double, rose-pink with white centre, free-flowering with large blooms, vigorous, semi-dwarf; 'Occold Embers', double, salmon-pink, golden yellow with bronze zone; 'Occold Shield', semi-double, orange-red, leaves have bronze 'shield' shape in centre; 'Rosina Read' (AGM), apple-blossom pink to cream, pale green zoned foliage; 'Rosita' (AGM), double, scarlet, one of the first dwarf rosebud types; 'Shelley', pale pink with irregular red markings; 'Silver Kewense', crimson, raised at Kew, very slow-growing, eventually reaching 20cm (8in), silver-leaved; 'Sugar Baby' (syn. 'Pink Gay Baby'), bright pink, second miniature ivy-leaved variety in England; 'Sun Rocket', brilliant orange-scarlet with paler reverse to petals, large flower heads and large floppy foliage, semi-dwarf; 'Tammy', semi-double, bright scarlet, pale green foliage with faint zone, fast growing; 'Turkish Delight', vermilion, tricolour, white stems often tinged with pink, a Canadian variety; 'Wendy Read', double, deep rose-pink, dark green zoned foliage.

MINIATURE PELARGONIUMS

" Much of what I said about the dwarf varieties also applies to the miniatures except that almost all of them are tiny Zonals. The effects of the dwarfing gene were known in the nineteenth century when the first varieties were bred. They are pretty little things and my only real regret is that there are so few miniature versions of the fancy-leaved varieties. The Rev. Stanley Stringer who bred the distinctive small 'Deacon' series (page 60) was responsible for many of the best modern miniatures and since his death, the flow of new forms has not been nearly as impressive. "

ORIGIN: Miniature pelargoniums have existed for about 100 years although most varieties available today have been bred since the Second World War. 'Red Black Vesuvius' (which used to be called simply 'Black Vesuvius' by virtue of its dark foliage), was one of the first, and was introduced in 1890.
SIZE: 13-20cm (5-8in).

AVAILABLE COLOUR RANGE

Orange, pinks, reds, purple and white.

SPECIAL FEATURES

There is a wide range of flower colour in both singles and doubles. The foliage is usually dark green. Grow them in 9cm (3in) pots in a greenhouse or conservatory or use them as neat edging in small beds, or in containers like window boxes.

Pelargonium 'L'Elegante'

Recommended Varieties

'Alde', salmon-pink with white eye, free-flowering, dark green foliage with distinct zone; 'Arizona', double, purple; 'Baby Bird Egg', white with pink speckles, slow-growing and difficult to propagate; 'Belinda Adams' (AGM), double, white but flushed with pink, large flowers; 'Brackenwood' (AGM), double, lavender-pink; 'Bridal Veil' (AGM), white, golden foliage with faint zone; 'Cariboo Gold' (AGM), scarlet, golden foliage with brown zone, a stellar type from Canada; 'Chieko', double, crimson-purple with dark green foliage; 'Crowfield', double, lilac-pink, dark green foliage with darker zone; 'Denebola', semi-double, violet-pink with white centre; 'Diane', double, soft salmon-pink shading deeper to the base of the petals, dark green lightly-zoned foliage; 'Dolphin', soft red to pale vermilion with white eye; 'Dwarf Miriam Basey' (syns. 'Dwarf Miriam Read', 'Miriam Basey'), white overlaid with red, deep green foliage, slow-growing; 'Eclipse', double, crimson, dark green foliage with black zone; 'Els', deep peach-pink, petals narrow and serrated; 'Francis Parrett' (AGM), double, bright lavender; 'Frills', double, soft coral-salmon, many narrow petals, dark green foliage; 'Goblin', double, scarlet, dark green foliage, fast grower, an American variety; 'Golden Chalice', powder pink with scarlet markings, small leaves with dark zone and yellow edge; 'Golden Fleece', double, soft rose-pink, golden-green foliage with bronze zone, frilled leaves; 'Grace Wells', fuchsia-pink with darker veins and white base to upper petals, large flowers, dark green foliage with darker zone; 'Greengold Kleine Liebling' (syn. 'Greengold Petit Pierre'), pale crimson with white centre, small flowers, yellow-green foliage with cream blotch; 'Heidi', double, white flaked carmine with deep pink edges; 'Janet Kerrigan', double, pale salmon-pink, zoned foliage; 'Jaunty', double, red with white base; 'Jayne Eyre', deep lavender, zoned foliage; 'Kleine Liebling' (syn. 'Petit Pierre'), pink, small flowers but free-flowering, some zoning of foliage; 'L'Elegante' (AGM), very pale mauve with purple veins, green and white foliage with

shades of pink, a dwarf ivy-leaved variety from 1868; 'La France' (AGM), semi-double, mauve, free-flowering (often listed in catalogues as ivy-leaved); 'Lachskönigin' (syn. 'Beauty of Eastbourne'), cerise-red; 'Lilac Gem', double, lilac, ivy-leaved variety; 'Madame Salleron' (AGM), no flowers, circular, bicolour, an old variety from 1840-50; 'Memento', double, light apricot-salmon, dark green foliage with distinct zones; 'Miss Wackles', double, deep red, large flowers, zoned foliage; 'Mrs Pat', salmon-pink, pale green foliage with brown blotch, stellar type; 'Orion', double, orange-red, deep green with slight zoning, compact, usually no taller than 13cm (5in); 'Phyllis Read', pastel-pink with white eye, large flowers; 'Playmate',

pink fading to cream at the tip of the petals and crimson at the centre, ragged flowers,small foliage; 'Red Black Vesuvius' (syn. 'Black Vesuvius'), bright scarlet, foliage almost black, slow-growing, one of the oldest miniatures; 'Red Ice', double, orange-red; 'Redondo', double, salmon-red, small dark green foliage; 'Rigel', double, scarlet, deep green foliage with slight zoning, compact; 'Royal Norfolk', double, red-purple, dark green zoned foliage; 'Snowflake', pure white; 'Sweet Sue', mandarin-red with white eye; 'Timothy Clifford', double, deep salmon-pink, dark green foliage, compact; 'Wood's Surprise' (syn. 'Marble Sunset'), double, pale lilac, cream and green foliage, ivy-leaved variety.

Pelargonium **'La France'**

Pelargonium **'Madame Salleron'**

SCENTED-LEAVED PELARGONIUMS

"I have to confess that, purely by chance, the further we progress through this book, the greater my fondness for the pelargonium categories grows. And with the scented-leaved forms we come close to my favourite type. To have a group of 20 or more varieties of these plants close together on the greenhouse bench on a warm evening, immediately after they have all been watered, is to experience an almost intoxicating blend of aromas. I suppose that spiciness prevails, but all those other wonderful plant fragrances, from roses to citrus have their pelargonium counterparts. But oddly enough, while I grow them in my greenhouse, where they are one of the largest groups of plants I collect, it is outside during the summer that so many friends admire them. For the scented-leaved pelargonium is kept too often solely indoors, people imagining that the garden is the domain of the Zonals and their like. Yet large pots, each containing perhaps half a dozen scented-leaved varieties (either planted directly into the compost or simply retained in their own individual pots and packed together) can be delightful if positioned close to a seat. I admit that most do not have the spectacular flowers of many of the other types of pelargonium, but their attractions are more than ample compensation.

I also have to admit that I always find a special attraction in plants that have been gracing gardens for centuries. I think this is why I am so fond of older varieties of roses (see Book 7 of the series, Best Roses*). Although by the 17th and eighteenth centuries, when the growing of pelargoniums first began, plants were being grown purely for their ornamental appeal, horticulture was still affected by the herbalist and the apothecary. And scented-leaved pelargoniums were so appealing because they have numerous herbal attractions. The foliage and the flowers can be used in salads or with cakes and other confectionery and the oils are highly prized for aromatherapy. You will gain much pleasure from experimenting with them in the kitchen though some scents will prove very much more satisfactory than others; do your experimenting before you inflict the flavour on your guests. The only one to avoid is the curiously scented 'Filicifolium' which is reputedly poisonous."*

Pelargonium **'Chocolate Peppermint'**

ORIGIN: These have been grown for about 300 years in herb and medicinal gardens so it is hard to distinguish true species from hybrids.

SIZE: Varies, depending mainly on the species from which they originated. Those I have listed below are small (30-45cm [12-18in]) unless I have stated otherwise, when I have referred to them as either medium (45-60cm [18-24in]) or tall (75-90cm [30-36in]).

AVAILABLE COLOUR RANGE

Pinks, reds, mauves, purples and white, but please don't judge them by their flowers. Always try to see and handle the foliage before making your choice.

SPECIAL FEATURES

Aromatic foliage when crushed and interesting leaf shape is the main attraction but some flower for a long time too. People's reactions to, and descriptions of, the aromas vary greatly so it is worth sampling before you buy rather than relying on catalogue descriptions. A warm day is the best to compare aromas. Use scented-leaved pelargoniums in mixed plantings, in containers or beds, especially if you want an informal effect. Being very tolerant of dry air, they are worth considering as foliage houseplants. They can grow rather large but are easily trimmed back. Grow in the garden besides paths or near a herb bed. Many of the scented-leaved species can be used in pot-pourri or in cooking.

LEFT: *Pelargonium* **'Lilian Pottinger'**

ABOVE: *Pelargonium* **'Lady Plymouth'**

Recommended Varieties

'Atomic Snowflake', bright mauve, rose scent, variegated green and cream, medium; 'Attar of Roses', mauve, rose scent, medium; 'Blandfordianum' (syn. *P. canescens*), white with red markings, rose scent, grey-green, tall if supported but can be allowed to trail; 'Brunswick', magenta-rose with red markings, large flowers, sweet scent, dark green, tall; 'Camphor Rose', rose-pink with darker markings, camphor rose scent, tall; 'Charmy Snowflake', mauve, lemon scent, medium; 'Chocolate Peppermint' (syns. 'Chocolate Tomentosum', *P. tomentosum* 'Chocolate Peppermint') (AGM), mauve, peppermint scent, large green leaves with dark blotch, tall; 'Citriodorum', dark mauve, lemon scent, grey-green, medium, but needs pinching out; 'Citronella', mauve, lemon scent, small rough leaves, bushy habit, very tall; 'Concolor Lace', bright rose-scarlet, free-flowering, nutmeg scent, compact; 'Copthorne' (AGM), mauve with dark blotch on upper petals, large flowers, cedar wood scent, medium; 'Creamy Nutmeg' (syn. Fragrans Group 'Creamy Nutmeg'), white, small flowers, pine scent, tightly curled leaves with cream markings, medium; 'Dark Lady', pale mauve, peppermint scent, grey-green; 'Deerwood Lavender Lad', magenta, lavender scent; 'Fair Ellen' (syn. *P. quercifolium* 'Fair Ellen'), pale pink with dark red markings, balsam scent, dark, compact; 'Filicifolium', sparse, small purple-pink flowers, a curious plant with coarse, very narrow, elongated toothed and slightly sticky leaves, usually said to be poisonous; 'Fragrans Variegatum', white, pine scent, variegated; 'Frensham', mauve, lemon scent, rough leaves, tall; 'Galway Star' (AGM), pale mauve, lemon scent, cream and green variegated, medium; 'Graveolens', pale pink, lemon-scent, tall; 'Grey Lady Plymouth', mauve,

Pelargonium **'Graveolens'**

rose scent, grey-green with cream splashes, medium; 'Lady Mary', deep mauve upper petals, pale mauve lower petals, faintly lemon scent, small leaves, medium; Lady Plymouth' (AGM), pale rose-pink, small flowers, lemon scent, variegated cream and green; 'Lady Scarborough' (syn. 'Countess of Scarborough'), rose-pink with purple veins, strawberry scent, tall; 'Lara Starshine', pink with mahogany markings, long flowering period, mild scent, bushy shape, a Unique hybrid; 'Lemon Fancy', mauve, lemon scent, tall; 'Lilian Pottinger', white, small flowers, nutmeg or pine scent, my favourite of all scented leaf varieties for its softly textured leaves, gentle fragrance and free production of pretty small flowers; 'Limoneum, mauve, sweet lime-rose scent, small leaves; 'Little Gem', mauve, small flowers, rose-lemon scent, feathery leaves, compact; 'Mabel Grey' (AGM), mauve, strong lemon scent, serrated leaves, tall; 'Madame Auguste Nonin' (syn. 'Monsieur Nonin'), rose-pink, paler at edges with cerise markings, sweet scent, medium; 'Old Spice', white, small flowers, spicy scent, compact; 'Pretty Polly', red, infrequent flowers, almond scent, compact; 'Prince of Orange', pale lavender with red-purple veins, free-flowering, orange scent, medium; 'Rober's Lemon Rose', mauve, rose lemon scent, grey-green, medium; 'Royal Oak', mauve, balsam scent, dark green, oak-shaped leaves, tall; 'Sweet Mimosa', pale pink, sweet scent, medium; 'Toronto', mauve, ginger scent, medium; Radula Group, pale purple, rose-lemon scent, medium.

For descriptions of aromatic species such as *P. capitatum*, *P. crispum* (including the very popular *P. crispum* 'Variegatum'), *P. grossularioides*, *P. odoratissimum* and *P. tomentosum* see page 90.

Pelargonium '**Royal Oak**'

Pelargonium '**Sweet Mimosa**'

IVY-LEAVED PELARGONIUMS

" As far as most gardeners are concerned, ivy-leaved varieties are the 'other' pelargoniums – the ones that are not Zonals. In reality, as readers will by now be aware, the genus is a diverse one and there are many other groups that are at least as distinctive in appearance. What the ivy-leaved varieties offer is a trailing habit, something that almost no other pelargoniums can rival. It is a stiff, angular trailing habit, but a trailing habit nonetheless. And this habit gave them a special role in hanging baskets and similar containers that was not threatened until the arrival of the 'Breakaway' type of Zonal in recent years. It has always struck me as curious that in Britain, where the hanging basket reaches a level of obsession that I think is not seen anywhere else, gardeners have always been conservative in the range of ivy-leaved varieties. I remember countless occasions in the past when people have returned from European holidays with small pieces of ivy-leaved pelargonium secreted in handbags and suitcases, having found far more varieties growing around Continental hotels than they had seen at home. Things have improved in recent times but I am still saddened that for most, it is necessary to go to specialist suppliers. Here surely is an area where garden centres and other popular plant outlets could take a lead and offer some of the lovely colours and doubles now available. "

Pelargonium **'Rouletta'**

ORIGIN: Bred from *P. peltatum* which scrambles through shrubs in its native habitat in the Cape Province of South Africa. Hybrid ivy-leaved varieties are the result of crosses between *P. peltatum* and zonals (*P. x hortorum*); they look like zonals but have a drooping habit. Some like 'Millfield Gem' (1894) are old, others like the 'Harlequins' were introduced in the 1980s.

SIZE: Varies greatly from long trailing plants up to 90cm (36in) to dwarf and miniature types.

AVAILABLE COLOUR RANGE

Generally white, pinks, mauves but also some reds and oranges.

SPECIAL FEATURES

The foliage has the appearance of an ivy (*Hedera*) and the leaf colour varies from a glossy dark green to variegated and some have attractive veins. Use them as single subjects for hanging baskets and window boxes, and in mild areas try training them against walls or other supports. The flowers and foliage are weather-tolerant, making these easy to grow and they are also have resistance to rust. Hybrid ivy-leaved types are best grown as pot plants.

ABOVE: 'Summer Showers'
RIGHT: *Pelargonium* 'Decora Lilas'

Pelargonium '**Hederinum Variegatum**'

Pelargonium '**Sybil Holmes**'

Recommended Varieties

'Amethyst' (syn. 'Hillscheider Amethyst') (AGM), semi-double, deep mauve, trailing; 'Audrey Clifton', semi-double, cerise-crimson with white centre, trailing; 'Barbe Bleu' (syn. 'Blue Beard'), double, purple black with lighter reverse; 'Belladonna', double, pink, successor to 'Galilee'; 'Blauer Frühling' (syn. 'Blue Spring'), double, mauve, hybrid ivy-leaved; 'Colonel Baden-Powell' (syn. 'Lord Baden-Powell'), double, blush-pink with maroon markings; 'Cornell', double, lavender with wine veins and serrated petals; 'Crocketta', white edged with crimson, semi-double, veined foliage; 'Elsi', double, crimson, green and cream variegated foliage; 'Enchantress', semi-double, soft rose-pink, early flowering, compact; 'Flakey' (AGM), double, pale mauve almost white, small flowers, green leaves streaked with white, miniature; 'Galilee' (AGM), double, bright rose-pink, flowers more weather resistant than most trailing varieties; 'Hederinum Variegatum' (syn. 'Duke of Edinburgh'), deep pink, variegated foliage; 'Icing Sugar', pale mauve-pink, very dwarf; 'Madame Crousse' (AGM), semi-double, pale pink; 'Magaluf', salmon-pink with crimson spots, variegated; 'Mexican Beauty', double, blood red; 'Millfield Gem', double, white with pale pink flush and a deeper blotch on the upper petals, hybrid ivy-leaved; 'Millfield Rose', double, pale pink, looks like rosebuds as it opens, hybrid ivy-leaved; 'Mrs W. A. R. Clifton', double, bright carnation-red; 'Pink Carnation', double, looks like a bright pink carnation thanks to red markings and serrated edges, indoor variety; 'Queen of Hearts', semi-double, white with deep pink markings, hybrid ivy-leaved; 'Renee Ross' (AGM), semi-double, rose-pink overlaid with coral-pink, upper petals have wine-red markings; 'Rhodamat' (AGM), double, light purple; 'Rigi', semi-double, deep cerise, vigorous; 'Rigoletto', double, darkest purple with white flush on petal; 'Rio Grande', double, almost black with white reverse; 'Roller's Pioneer', semi-double, deep burgundy, veined foliage; 'Rouletta' (syn. 'Mexicanerin'), semi-double, white with crimson edges; 'Santa Paula', rich mauve, compact; 'Schneekönigin' (syn. 'Snow Queen'), double, white with purple markings on upper petals; 'Super Rose', semi-double, rose-pink with darker markings; 'Sybil Holmes', double, bright pink rosebud flowers, free-flowering; 'Tavira', semi-double, light crimson; 'The Crocodile' (syn. 'Crocodile'), bright pink, veined foliage; 'White Mesh' (syn. 'Sussex Lace'), semi-double, light pink, one of the first veined-foliage varieties to be introduced; 'Yale' (AGM), semi-double, deep crimson.

Pelargonium **'Millfield Gem'**

Harlequin Series These are ivy-leaved pelargoniums with bicoloured flowers. They were introduced by Dennis Magson, a commercial grower in Kent in the 1980s. He grafted small pieces of 'Rouletta' on to other varieties such as 'Rigi' to transfer the white colour to them. The successful ones were called Harlequins. There are seven varieties of which 'Harlequin Mahogany' is the most striking, a semi-double with flowers of deep crimson and white.

Continental ivy-leaved varieties
From the early 1970s onwards these became popular in Europe for window boxes and hanging baskets; they are also known as balcony geraniums and look particularly impressive from a distance because they produce hundreds of single flowers. They are easy to grow and are 'self-cleaning' which means the flowers drop off as they fade so there is no need for deadheading. The more vigorous types trail to 60-90cm (24-36in) but the compact varieties such as the 'Mini Cascades' from Fischer of Germany only grow to 45cm (18in). Their flowers are closer together and they produce more of a mass of colour. 'Decora Lilas' (syns. 'Decora Mauve', 'Lila Compakt-Cascade'), lavender-pink, vigorous; 'Decora Rose' (syn. 'Sofie'), pale pink, vigorous; 'Decora Rouge', deeper pink than 'Decora Rose', vigorous; 'Hederinum' (syns. 'Balcon Rose', 'Roi des Balcons', 'Roi des Balcons Rose', 'King of Balcon', 'Ville de Paris', 'Pink Cascade'), light salmon-pink. 'Roi des Balcons Lilas' (syn. 'Lilac Cascade'), lilac; 'Rose Mini-Cascade' (syn. 'Pink Mini-Cascade'), rose-pink, compact; 'Rote Mini-Cascade' (syn. 'Red Mini-Cascade'), scarlet, compact.

Ivy-leaved varieties from seed
'Summer Showers' (five shades of purple, pink and red) was the first ivy-leaved pelargonium to be available for raising from seed. It was bred in the United States and when it was first produced it was awarded a Fleuroselect Silver medal but the general view is that this seemed to reflect a breeding achievement rather than a particularly attractive plant. The flowers are somewhat sparse and spidery and although these plants do have an appeal they fall far short of the traditional ivy-leaved pelargoniums propagated from cuttings. More recently, rather better varieties have become available, including the single-coloured 'Felix' (deep pink), 'Leo' (deep carmine red), 'Sheba' (white with pink markings) and 'Summertime Lilac' (pale lilac). More may be expected.

REGAL PELARGONIUMS

" *Put a regal pelargonium beside a scented-leaf variety such as 'Lilian Pottinger' and you will begin to appreciate the breadth of flower form the genus offers, because there is nothing small, delicate or frail about the flowers of a regal. They are big and bold. However, unlike other flowers that are big and bold (dahlias, chrysanthemums and begonias come to mind), they could never be described as 'brassy'. Their salvation is the feature that gives superficially similar flowers like gloxinias their special appeal – they have a texture that is best described as velvety, and they combine this with a colour range that is noble too, and never brash. Although the name regal came from a royal connection, it is altogether appropriate. In appearance, there is no question that these are the most royal-looking of any pelargonium. The only disadvantage of regals is that they are not good outdoor plants except in the hottest and driest of seasons. The big flowers and velvety texture are their downfall, soaking up rain like a sponge and leading to their swift demise.* "

Pelargonium **'Askham Fringed Aztec'**

ORIGIN: *P. cucullatum* is thought to be one of the principal parents of the regals (*P. x domesticum*). *Pelargonium cucullatum* however is carmine red; the colour range today is much wider than this and the white came from *Pelargonium grandiflorum*, purple from *Pelargonium angulosum* and a different, brighter red from *Pelargonium fulgidum*. The Regals were very popular in Victorian times but most varieties available today have been raised since the Second World War. Modern types tend to be grown for their compact habit and free-flowering abilities. The name 'Regal' is thought to originated around 1877 from their popularity in the royal gardens at Sandringham and Windsor; in the United States they are known as Martha Washingtons.
SIZE: 30-45 cm (12-18 in)

AVAILABLE COLOUR RANGE

Orange, pinks, purple, reds and white.

SPECIAL FEATURES

The azalea-like velvety flowers are impressive and most have attractive feather markings on the upper petals. They are relatively low, bushy plants that flower in spring before the zonals. The flowers are delicate, so grow them in pots in a greenhouse or as house-plants, they really are not good out-doors. Check regularly for whitefly and remove and destroy any yellowing leaves. The foliage is rather coarse and might be thought unattractive to them. Sadly, this isn't so.

Pelargonium 'Fringed Aztec'

Pelargonium 'Joy'

Pelargonium 'Lord Bute'

Recommended Varieties

'Askham Fringed Aztec' (AGM), white with purple markings, fringed petals; 'Aztec' (AGM), white with pink and brown markings, large flowers; 'Black Knight', purple-black edged with lavender, small flowers (sometimes listed as a 'decorative'); 'Bodey's Picotee', deep purple with white edge; 'Botley Beauty', crimson-purple with white edge; 'Bredon' (AGM), wine-red, large flowers, bushy; 'Brown's Butterfly' (syn. 'Black Butterfly'), black with mahogany flecks, an extra-ordinary and striking little plant; 'Bushfire' (AGM), bright red with dark blaze on petals; 'Carisbrooke' (AGM), pale pink with crimson markings, large flowers; 'Cezanne', pale lavender, almost white with purple markings, compact; 'Cherry Orchard', cherry-red with white throat, compact; 'Dark Secret', deep mahogany with burgundy markings; 'Dark Venus', dark mahogany; 'Doris Frith', white with occasional purple flecks; 'Eileen Postle' (AGM), wine-red edged with pale lavender and dark burgundy markings; 'Fareham' (AGM), purple and lilac with picotee edge; 'Fifth Avenue', purple-black; 'Fringed Aztec' (AGM), same as 'Aztec' but with fringed petals; 'Gemma Jewel' (AGM), upper petals deep cerise, lower petals lavender, large flowers; 'Georgina Blythe' (AGM), pale pink with white throat and purple veins; 'Glenshee', pale pink with red markings; 'Grand Slam', rose-red with red markings; 'Green Woodpecker', white with hint of lilac and maroon markings; 'Harbour Lights', upper petals dark salmon-pink, lower petals light pink, compact; 'Harewood Slam', deep cherry-red with darker markings; 'Hazel Birkby', deep rose-red with

Pelargonium **'Cezanne'**

dark crimson markings, compact, one of many in the 'Hazel' series, particularly good as houseplants; 'Honeywood Lindy', white with a pink spot on each petal; 'Inca', upper petals deep red, lower petals salmon-pink, dwarf and bushy; 'Joan Morf', white shading to rose-pink, ruffled petals; 'Joy' (AGM), pink-red with white throat, ruffled petals, small flowers on vigorous plant; 'Julia' (AGM), upper petals deep maroon, lower petals deep pink, compact; 'Lamorna', cerise-scarlet with pink throat and wine-red markings; 'Lavender Grand Slam' (AGM), lavender; 'Lord Bute' (AGM), purple-black edged with wine-red, one of the oldest varieties from 1910; 'Miss Australia', clear pink, variegated foliage (sometimes listed as a 'decorative' pelargonium); 'Morwenna', deep wine-red to black; 'Noche', deep mahogany edged with coral-red; 'Phyllis Richardson', double, rose-pink; 'Pink Bonanza', pale salmon-pink with white throat, large flowers; 'Rembrandt', royal purple shading to lavender at the edges with white eye; 'Royal Ascot', deep crimson with white throat (often listed as a decorative); 'Sefton' (AGM), cerise-red with wine-red markings; 'South American Bronze' (AGM), bronze with a narrow picotee margin of white; 'Strawberry Sundae', strawberry-pink with white centre; 'Sunrise', salmon-orange with white throat, large flowers; 'Vicky Claire', upper petals deep red with white edge, lower petals white with pink markings; 'White Chiffon', white; 'White Glory' (AGM), white sometimes slightly marked with red, very bushy; 'Yhu', deep crimson with white edge, small flowers on a vigorous plant.

Pelargonium 'Joan Morf'

PELARGONIUM SPECIES

" *Probably because my early training was in botany rather than horticulture, I have a soft spot for species, and this is true for almost all genera, from* Pelargonium *to* Fuchsia. *I love the diversity that nature offers, without human intervention and I love the simplicity of the natural flower. Not far from where I live is a nursery that houses one of the National Collections of* Pelargonium *and whenever I visit, I am fascinated by the comments of other visitors, many of whom are quite unaware of what* Pelargonium *species are, and are totally entranced by them. They will not produce flowers of the size, or quantity, or with the frequency of the garden varieties but that is a small price to pay for seeing the beauty that nature can offer. My problem has been choosing my recommendations from the total number, and I have limited myself to those with which I am most familiar, that succeed best in a temperate climate, and that are regularly available, at least from specialist nurseries. I have grouped them according to the various sub-divisions of the genus.* "

Sub-genus *Reniformia*

ORIGIN: Found in southern Cape Province. These areas receive more rain in summer and winter than the more desert-like areas further north although the habitat is still rocky and dry. *P. odoratissimum* is found over large areas of southern and eastern Africa, often in shady spots under bushes. Most species have been cultivated for around 200 years for their aromatic foliage.
SIZE: Varies greatly depending on the species.

AVAILABLE COLOUR RANGE

White, pale pink or bright purple-pink.

SPECIAL FEATURES

Herbaceous or woody plants with aromatic foliage. A long flowering period but the flowers, which have an irregular shape are sparse. They make good houseplants, given a light position and careful watering.

Recommended Species:
P. abrotanifolium, white but pink forms sometimes found, grey-green foliage that is deeply divided, a branching, straggly habit up to 50cm (20in) tall with woody stems; *P. dichondrifolium*, white with red markings, short woody stem up to 20cm (8in) tall, long petioles remain on the plant making it look untidy; *P. exstipulatum*, pale pink with red markings, a small woody shrub up to 1m (3ft) but less in a container, sticky grey-green foliage; *P. odoratissimum*, white with red markings, bright green foliage usually with an apple scent, low-growing plant but with trailing flower stems up to 50cm (20in) long which can be cut back after flowering; *P. reniforme*, bright pink to magenta with darker veins, shrubby habit with grey-green foliage, tuberous roots.

Sub-genus *Ciconium*

ORIGIN: *P. acetosum* is found in the eastern part of Cape Province in an area of summer rainfall. It has been cultivated in Holland and England since the early 1700s. *P. alchemilloides* is found over a wide area of southern and eastern Africa. *P. peltatum* is often found scrambling through shrubs; it grows not only in the winter rainfall zone of Cape Province but extends east into Natal and the eastern Transvaal. It was introduced into Europe in 1700 and grown in England a year later by the Duchess of Beaufort. *P. quinquelobatum* is found from Tanzania and Kenya to Ethiopia. *P. tongaense* was named as recently as 1983 after an area in Natal where it grows in humid, shady places.
SIZE: Varies with the species.

Pelargonium gibbosum

Pelargonium odoratissimum

AVAILABLE COLOUR RANGE

White, pink, pink-purple or red depending on the species. *P. quinquelobatum* has unusually coloured flowers of grey, blue and yellow.

SPECIAL FEATURES

Large plants, often with fleshy stems. Easy to grow. Within this group are the parents both of the zonal pelargoniums (*P. zonale* and *P. inquinans*) and the ivy-leaved pelargoniums (*P. peltatum*) worth having for their historical interest.

Recommended Species:
P. acetosum, pale pink with narrow petals, brittle stems reaching to 60cm (24in), blue-green succulent foliage tasting of sorrel; *P. alchemilloides*, white, cream or pink, low-growing hairy plant 10 x 12cm (4 x 5in), foliage often zoned; *P. peltatum*, white to pale purple to pink, a variable plant with a trailing or climbing habit that can reach 2m (7ft) in the wild, ivy-shaped leaves; *P. quinquelobatum*, grey-blue-yellow, dull green foliage with a blue tinge, hairy plant growing to 30cm (12in); *P. tongaense*, bright red, similar to *P. peltatum*, attractive and easy to grow in sun or shade. Although I've only grown this for a short time, I think it is the most shade tolerant *Pelargonium* I know.

Sub-genus *Peristera*

ORIGIN: *P. australe* is found in Australia, Tasmania and New Zealand. A variable species found in a range of habitats from sand dunes to cultivated land. *P. grossularioides* is widely distributed in southern Africa and has been cultivated since 1731. It has become naturalised in parts of California where its lack of hardiness is not a problem.
SIZE: 30cm (12in).

Pelargonium peltatum

AVAILABLE COLOUR RANGE
White with red streaks, pink, dark purple-pink.

SPECIAL FEATURES
Annuals or short-lived perennials with small flowers. Best grown in light, well-drained composts.

Recommended Species:
P. australe, white with red streaks or pink, habit initially compact but with straggly flowering stems up to 30cm (12in); *P. grossularioides*, dark purple-pink, red-tinged stems, trailing habit, aromatic foliage with a fruity scent.

Sub-genus *Pelargonium*

ORIGIN: Most are from the winter rainfall regions of southern Cape Province and are found in coastal areas or near streams, even if these dry up for part of the year. *P. capitatum* often grows in sand dunes and was one of the earliest species imported into Europe; records reveal that it was brought into England from Holland in 1690 by Hans Willem Bentinck. Many other species in this group have been cultivated in Europe since the early 18th century: *P. crispum*, the familiar lemon-scented pelargonium, which originates in the south-western Cape and has been cultivated since 1774, *P. cucullatum* which was probably one of the original parents of the regal pelargoniums, and *P. tomentosum* which grows in the mountain areas at the edge of forests of south-western Cape Province.
SIZE: Can become large and quite woody, but in cultivation mostly 1m (3ft) or less.

AVAILABLE COLOUR RANGE
White or shades of pink or purple.

SPECIAL FEATURES
Included within this group are the parents of scented-leaved varieties, angels, uniques and regals. Many have aromatic foliage; all are easy to grow if given a light position and a well-drained soil. *P. tomentosum* can be grown in partial shade in moist positions. All can be planted outside after the last frosts.

Recommended Species:

P. capitatum, mauve-pink, hairy, rose-scented foliage but some types have less scent so check before buying, a spreading plant reaching 1m (3ft), stems tend to become woody at the base; *P. citronellum*, pale pink-mauve with purple markings, lemon-scented foliage, pinch out shoot tips to encourage branching; *P. crispum*, pink flowers with darker pink markings, a coarse-leaved shrubby plant with a strong lemon fragrance, one of the most popular house-plant pelargoniums and probably the parent of several scented-leaf varieties, the variety 'Variegatum' has cream edges to the leaves; *P. cucullatum*, bright purple-pink, large flowers, hairy shrub over 2m (7ft) in

the wild, cup-shaped foliage, sometimes with a red margin and aromatic; *P. papilionaceum*, light to dark pink, attractive flowers shaped like a butterfly, hairy shrub to over 2m (7ft) in the wild, foliage has unpleasant smell; *P. quercifolium*, pale pink to dark purple-pink with darker markings, balsam-scented foliage, vigorous shrub to more than 1.5m (5ft) in the wild; *P. radens*, pink-purple, rose or lemon-scented foliage, finely-divided foliage rough to the touch; *P. tomentosum* (AGM), white sometimes tinged with pale purple, soft velvety foliage with a peppermint scent, lower growing than many, to about 60cm (24in) and a very important plant in my summer containers.

lower ones. *P. endlicherianum* can be grown in an alpine house or outdoors on a rock garden in sunny, dry places sheltered from excess rain. *P. tetragonum* has angled green succulent stems with few leaves. These stems allow the plant to survive even when the leaves have fallen in the dry season.

Recommended Species:

P. endlicherianum, bright purple-pink, rosette of leaves, reaches 20cm (8in); *P. tetragonum*, cream or pale pink with dark red veins, large flowers, brittle succulent stems are easy to root.

Sub-genus *Polyactium*

ORIGIN: West coast of South Africa where it scrambles through shrubs. Grown in England since 1712.
SIZE: Scrambles for several metres in the wild.

AVAILABLE COLOUR RANGE

Green-yellow flowers.

SPECIAL FEATURES

Known as the gouty pelargonium due to the swollen-jointed nodes on the stem. Spreading plant with succulent stems. The stems are brittle and are best kept supported but root easily if bits are broken off. Flowers are particularly sweetly-scented at night. I have seen this plant making an attractive feature when given more or less free rein in a warm conservatory.

Pelargonium quercifolium

Sub-genus *Jenkinsonia*

ORIGIN: *P. endlicherianum* originates from rocky mountainous areas in Turkey and first flowered at Kew in 1856. *P. tetragonum* is from South Africa. Both grow in regions with very hot dry summers and winter rainfall.
SIZE: *P. endlicherianum* 20cm (8in); *P. tetragonum* 35cm (14in).

AVAILABLE COLOUR RANGE

Pinks, purple, white.

SPECIAL FEATURES

The flowers have two large upper petals and two or three much smaller

INDEX

INDEX

PHOTOGRAPHIC ACKNOWLEDGMENTS

All photos in this book have been specially commissioned from
Andrew Lawson with the exception of the following:

A-Z Botanical Collection /A Stenning 34, /Anthony Seinet 56
Eric Crichton 29
Garden Picture Library /JS SIRA 46 left
John Glover 44 left, 44 right
Reed Consumer Books Ltd. /Jerry Harpur 33, /George Wright 24
David Hibberd 25 top, 45
Andrew Lawson Photography 5, 22, 40, 41 bottom, 65, 66 left, 66 right, 72 left, 72 right, 76, 77 right, 79 top, 80, 81 left, 83 right, 90, 91, 93
Photos Horticultural Back jkt, 23 top, 27 left, 30 left, 37 left, 39 top, 43, 55 top, 57 right, 57 left, 74 top, 75, 83 left, 86
Harry Smith Collection 31, 55 bottom

With special thanks to the following who allowed their gardens to be photographed:
Martin & Eva Bourcier, Docton Mill, Hartland, Devon; Kirsty & Hector Christie, Tapeley Park, Bideford, Devon; Country Life Garden, RHS Chelsea Flower Show 1997; East Lambrook Manor, Somerset; Fibrex Nurseries, Pebworth, Warwickshire; The Garden House, Buckland, Monachorum, Devon; Gothic House, Charlbury, Oxford; John & Antoinette Moat, Hartland, Devon; Wendy & Michael Perry, Bosvigo House Garden, Truro, Cornwall; RHS Chelsea Flower Show 1997; RHS Gardens, Rosemoor, Devon; Royal Botanic Garden, Kew; Kathy & Roy Taylor, Addisford Cottage, Dolton, Devon; University Botanic Gardens, Oxford; Rosemary Verey, Barnsley House, Glos.